THE AUTHO

Although all three authors have worked on this book in total collaboration, they have contributed to this evaluation of Zia regime in Pakistan through their own unique understanding of the country, and the issues involved.

Anthony Hyman is a journalist with many years of experience in the field and specialises in South Asian and Middle-Eastern affairs. He has travelled through the region extensively and his book AFGHANISTAN UNDER SOVIET DOMINATION 1964-83 was published by Macmillan in 1984.

Muhammed Ghayur is a seasoned Pakistani journalist who now lives in London. He was a stringer for the BBC from 1969 to 1977 when he joined their Urdu service. Currently he writes and broadcasts as a freelance.

Naresh Kaushik started his journalistic career with the Times of India group in India and has been working as a producer on the staff of the Hindi Service of the BBC since 1981. He has written extensively on South Asian affairs for many journals in India.

ACKNOWLEDGEMENTS

The Publishers and the Writers of this book would like to express their heartfelt gratitude to many people for their encouragement and helpful advice, both before, and especially during, the rapid preparation of this book, who have actively or racitly helped to make this publication possible, either by giving their benign support, time and advice, or by lending materials.

Very special mention must be made of

Mr David Page, Assistant Head of the Eastern Service of the BBC.

Mr H.V.S. Manral, First Secretary, Information & Press, India House, London.

Mr Muhammad Sorwar, the News Editor of Daily Jong, London.

Mr Zubeir Ali, Information Minister at the Pakistan Embassy, London.

And most of all, our respective wives who missed us throughout this operation and were good enough not to misunderstand us.

However, our gratitude must not in any way be construed as though statements were fed to us. In fact, the research is our own and so are all the opinions and conclusions. We stand by them.

i

PAKISTAN:
ZIA AND AFTER . . .

Anthony Hyman
Muhammed Ghayur
Naresh Kaushik

ASIA PUBLISHING HOUSE
London

First Published in Great Britain by
ASIA PUBLISHING HOUSE 1988

ASIA PUBLISHING HOUSE
(a division of BOOKS FROM INDIA UK LIMITED)
45 Museum Street, London WC1A 1LR

ISBN 0 948724 12 9

British Library Cataloguing in Publication Data

Hyman, Anthony
Pakistan: Zia and after —
1. Pakistan. Zia-ul-Haq Mohammed, 1924-1988.
I. Title. II. Ghayur, Muhammed. III. Kaushik, Naresh 954.9 105 0924.

ISBN 0 948724 12 9

Printed and Typeset in Great Britain by Premier Printing, Sittingbourne, Kent.

iv

Contents

Illustrations

THIS BOOK

General Zia was a nobody. General Zia staged a coup and crowned himself a President. Then he hanged his erstwhile mentor, ignoring all the pleas of clemency from the world leaders, and became a pariah in the comity of nations.

Question that everyone should ask, and perhaps is asking, is what transpired that turned him into the darling of the West and gave him the status of "a bastion of freedom"? Is this phenomena liable to repeat itself in the Third World, and if so, why? Is it merely the result of the Super power intervention, seeking "stability" in their respective spheres of influence, or are there also elements at home that breed this kind of dictator and bring them to power?

These are some of the questions that this book asks and tries to answer, in the context of the facts on ground, in Pakistan and in the territories around.

Cover Designed by
ANURĀG

A Publisher's Panic

It was 17th of August. I was working late in my office and the small, black-and-white television set on my office table was switched on, purely to keep generating some background noise and create around me a sense of company. It happens at home to most of us: we just switch these damned boxes on instinctively when we reach our sitting rooms, and rarely pay any attention to what is being shown or said, especially at the news time.

However, in this case, I was suddenly alerted by a sudden dip in the voice of the newscaster and a long narrative of the chronology in the recent history of Pakistan came into my focus of hearing. I had already missed out the headline, but my suspicion − a catastrophe had struck either Pakistan or her General-President − was confirmed at the end of the bulletin when the headlines were repeated.

I personally am a refugee from what became West Pakistan in 1947, and a Hindu. But having been in journalism for 30-odd years, and having observed the political upheavals of this century, I have become sort of immune from the personal and emotional trauma of that partition of India. I have become more intensely aware of the real issues that confront the people of India and Pakistan, irrespective of the issues of immediate nationality of religious differences.

This awareness and concern for the real issues and the perennial interests of the people of Pakistan, as much as of India, has always been there. But this news bulletin stunned me beyond anything I had ever experienced before. I was possessed with a strange sense of urgency and need for quick assessment as to what had happened in the past eleven years, whether it was purely a continuation of earlier trends or had ushered in a significant new element into the drama being played out there, whether it was time that Pakistan took stock of her problems and struck a new course or whether that country − like to many others around the globe − had forever become a helpless pawn in the geographical game being played by the superpowers, whether Islam in Pakistan was going to be able to bring the Muslim world into the 20th century or were the followers of that noble faith forever doomed to live within the savage confines of the Middle-Ages, and many more questions. It is another thing that, like all politicians, the politicians and generals in Pakistan had wasted opportunities for democratic development which were afforded to them.

I couldn't make this assessment by myself. And yet, being a publisher. I had a role to play. I must play this role.

That night these questions haunted me and I couldn't sleep. Next morning, I offered my first tribute to that country by displaying in my shop-window all the books on Pakistan that I could lay my hands on, around a copy of THE TIMES carrying the banner headline news of President Zia's death.

At about 9 a.m. that morning (August 18, 1988), I started ringing around and tracking down journalists who could and would undertake the job of writing a book, on Pakistan and President Zia's rule and his impact.

Many phone calls, agitated conversations and constant awareness of the need to present a factual, lively and yet balanced picture, brought a team of three writers together.

We held our first meeting at 11 a.m., August 19 in my office where the broad outlines of the book were discussed and a consensus was developed with regard to the aspects and topics to be analysed. It was decided by the writers that they would discuss the title for the book over lunch that day.

At 4.30 p.m. Naresh Kaushik phoned me and gave me the title which all these usually had agreed upon. I immediately sat down to type out the news release which was sent out to various trade and public media, in Britain, in India and in Pakistan.

Next morning, about 11 a.m. I set about, from home base, over the telephone, contacting all three writers of the book so as to give them the operational details: how was the copy-flow to be started and maintained so that the editors could edit and instruct the typesetters, how the printers were to be fed with camera-ready-copy so that they could shoot and print, who was to design the cover, whose name was to go into acknowledgements, and a few dozen other problems which have to be tackled in the course of publishing a book.

I was on the phone, all day Saturday and Sunday (August 20 and 21, 1988) commissioning services and making necessary connections. For some unknown reason, one of the three writers could not be contacted. Even Monday went by and there was no connection made with him. Tuesday, all day, went the same way; no contact.

On Tuesday evening, an unpalatable decision was taken, with the consent of the other two; we had to replace the missing writer in order to bring the team to full strength and we could not afford to waste any time.

Muhammed Ghayur was taken on board then. And it goes to his credit that he agreed to undertake the job at such short notice.

My job as publisher had barely begun: I still had to find a typesetter, an overall editor/proof reader, and a printer who would undertake the job and deliver copies of the book on time.

Premier Printing people could not undertake the typesetting as well as the printing job within the time scale we had in mind. We were faced with the question whether dispensing with the furniture-value of the typefaces would

xii

expedite the operation and hard copy generated by our in-house wordprocessor on the desktop daisey wheel printer could be used to shoot-and-print. Time was of the essence.

In the course of doing all this, our budgets escalated beyond recognition. We had already made the advance announcement, on the basis of authors' fees as agreed and editorial costs as fixed and printer's charges as guessed. We were surprised to find that when you are pressed for time, your room to manouvre on prices of goods and services radically shrinks to minimum.

The difficulty was that on the basis of intial guesswork, and on the basis of my bookselling experience and the estimated price of the book we had already declared our retail price to the trade and now, whatever the escalation in the cost of production, we had to stick to the declared price.

On Monday, the 22nd of August, the editor of the Publishing News phoned me to confirm the publication and fill in some details, and assured me that the news item was going in the first available issue. We were now committed.

Till the afternoon of the 24th, our authors were still huddled into conference sessions and not a word had been scribbled by any one of them. I was reminding them of the printers' deadline (Premier Printing of Sittingbourne had agreed to take on the job provided we could deliver to them a camera-ready-copy by Tuesday, the 30th) and they kept nodding their heads indicating the impossibility thereof.

The search for relevant photographs was another headache. We could not afford to go to Fleet Street photo agencies (money being in short supply) and the Pakistan Embassy had no material available in stock. They were willing to try to obtain some from Islamabad but we couldn't wait that long.

Indian High Commission was tried. The first attempt came to nothing. Three days later, a second attempt got us one good photograph.

Muhammed Ghayur suggested that I try approaching Jang daily (Urdu) in London. Mr Sarwar of that blessed newspaper was most forthcoming. He promised to loan us some pictures if we were to put in a written request. We did and he obliged.

But what he provided us with was neither sufficient nor up to the highest standard.

Young Anurag, my elder son, in spite of his very heavy commitments to SPORTAID 88 (which was approaching its climax), agreed to use his graphic vision and design a cover for the book. We sat through to 2 a.m. on Saturday night (September 3) to finalise the design work and layout.

The CIP office of the British Library were most helpful in granting the CATALOGUING-IN-PUBLICATION DATA within a couple of hours in view of our urgent request.

About a third of the text of the book was delivered to me, by the three authors, after their consensus building conference, on the evening of Tuesday, the 30th August and was handed over to the printers.

But this delivery was made with a built-in delay in the maturing of the entire project. We were running late and there was no time for our in-house wordprocessor to generate the hard copy of a high enough standard to shoot and print. Premier were asked, at the spur of the moment to do the typesetting as well.

A week later, when the entire copy of the main text was delivered to the printers, and they were good enough to set it all in a couple of days, we were writing and designing the final layout and look of the book, and they were ringing up and down the country in search of a perfect-binder willing to undertake sewing of 16-page sections, and able to deliver at least a third of the print-run in good time.

Today is the 8th of September and the printer's ultimatum is, "cease in-putting new material and design-work or accept delay of another week." We can't afford the delay. So we have to forego all delusions of aesthetically sound production: we must accept that we are going for a readable and authentic analysis of a highly complex political subject. Other considerations have to be abandoned.

Therefore, even I have to call it a day so that the printers can print, the binders can bind and the readers can read, assuming that, in between somewhere, the post-office workers of the Royal Mail currently on strike will go back to work, the booksellers will receive supplies and manage to sell, and an occasional reviewer will find it worth his while to reveiw the book.

EVAMASTU (Let it be so).

Shreeram Vidyarthi

1

Assassination

A small group of the most powerful people in Pakistan were relaxing aboard a C-130 Hercules transport plane. It was mid-afternoon on 17 August 1988, and the VIPs confidently expected a short routine flight of seventy minutes back to Islamabad, the capital of Pakistan.

Shortly after take-off from Bahawalpur, though, the aircraft was rocked by a powerful explosion. Within seconds the plane was engulfed in fire, exploding in mid-air. Everyone aboard was killed, their bodies burned so badly as to be almost unrecognisable.

President Zia-ul-Haq had gone to this southern part of the Punjab, close to the border with India, so it was said, to watch a display of new US-made M1 tanks.

In the party were thirty people, including the US ambassador to Pakistan, Arnold Raphel, and senior Pakistani officers, including some of Zia's closest military aides, General Akhtar Abdul Rahman, Chairman of Joint Chiefs of Staff, and Lt-General Mohammad Afzal, Chief of Army General Staff.

Rumours of the plane crash had swept the cities hours before Pakistan radio belatedly announced the death of the country's President that evening, at 8pm. The crash had occurred, by a curious twist of fate, near the General's birthplace in Jullundur, in the Indian part of Punjab.

Zia had survived numerous attempts at assassination since 1977. Security measures were exhaustive and usually judged highly efficient. However, Zia had reportedly become nervous of attempts on his life during the summer months. This was, at any rate, one of few trips the well-travelled General had made out of Islamabad since early summer.

On previous trips Zia had used this same transport plane bearing military markings. Sturdy, super-reliable but noisy, the C-130 had been made more homely by the addition of a settee for the President's comfort.

Before the take off from Islamabad airport, the plane had been given a thorough check against sabotage by metal detectors and electric scanning devices. How

THE DEATH OF PRESIDENT ZIA

THE REGIONAL CRISIS

Afghanistan first to feel the impact

By Karan Thapar

● **Pressure may grow for early elections to fill the vacuum** ●

● **Mujahidin could face considerable political setback** ●

General Zia: Violent end to an 11-year era of machiavellian manoeuvring.

THE COUNTRY

Violent tradition claimed former leaders

By Paul Vallely

CARETAKER LEADER

Senate chairman takes over helm

From Zahid Hussain, Karachi

THE MAN AND HIS MIND

Subtle general outmanoeuvred his foes

By Anatol Lieven

Challenge on election

WASHINGTON'S REGIONAL EXPERT

Raphael was key diplomat in Asian affairs

From Charles Bremner, New York

Mr Ghulam Ishaq Khan: Close to seat of power since 1977.

WHO WILL FILL THE VACUUM?

Choices are elections, followed by Bhutto, or more of the Army

By Tariq Ali

Miss Bhutto: Her future could lie in Britain a few years ago.

2

had the bomb been smuggled on the plane amid such tight security? The weak link in security could have come from the standard practise for presidential trips of loading containers with chairs and other items of furniture, stored in airport hangers. Investigators' suspicions centred on a possible breach in security at Bahawalpur. Crates of mangoes were loaded onto the plane at Bahawalpur, presented before takeoff by local dignitaries, which apparently escaped checks.

Rigorous investigations went on immediately into all the staff of all grades at the two airports, with hundreds taken in for questioning.

Zia's death was surely no accident. But pinning responsibility for it with complete certainty is, at the time of writing, far from straight forward. To plant an explosive device amid such tight security, there must have been involvement in the plot by dissident officers, mechanics or other personnel within Pakistan's armed forces.

Of the various theories current, by far the most probable one seems to be that the action was carried out, or at least aided by agents of KHAD, (the Afghan intelligence service).

KHAD already had an extensive network in Pakistan, where it has carried out hundreds of terrorist bombings in recent years. In left-wing circles of Pakistan's domestic opposition, the Kabul regime is often regarded with great favour. Several thousand Pakistanis have become exiles in Afghanistan since 1978, some of them working closely with or for KHAD.

The assassination of Pakistan's strongman by Soviet KGB agents was ruled out by most observers. Since the KGB itself created, and still directs the activities of KHAD, direct Soviet involvement would anyway be superfluous. Quite a number of analysts saw, though − with the benefit of hindsight − a special significance in the series of emphatic Russian warnings delivered from the end of May 1988, of "very serious consequences", if Pakistan continued to service the arms pipeline to the Afghan guerrillas.

Among the Pakistani public, reactions to the death varied greatly. On the surface, at least, people in the cities took the news calmly. Across the Indian border in Srinagar and other towns, in the disputed Muslim-majority territory of Kashmit, Muslim crowds used the death as an excuse for demonstrations the next day, put down by police shootings.

In Pakistan, ten days of official mourning were ordered for the death of General Zia. The well-attended state funeral in Islamabad was a relatively low-key affair. There were no large demonstrations, and if there was grief, it was mostly private. There were some celebrations too.

Zia was undoubtedly a highly controversial man. The 64 year-old military

3

dictator of Pakistan had effectively ruled Pakistan for eleven years, ruling for much of it under harsh martial laws. A devout, God-fearing Muslim, Zia had rather dogmatic views on the type of society Pakistan should become. Zia had made many enemies from Pakistan's opposition parties. Yet these had no expertise to carry out such an act of terrorism, requiring careful coordination and sophisticated planning. Only one perhaps had the necessary experience − Al-Zulfikar, the small group of Pakistani dissidents based in Kabul, and headed from 1979 by the two sons of Pakistan's hanged Prime Minister Zulfikar Ali Bhutto. Al-Zulfikar was explicitly dedicated to getting revenge for Bhutto's death.

The Al-Zulfikar group did carry out a missile attack on General Zia's plane in 1982. The missile failed to hit the target, though, and the attempt was made the excuse for a harh and effective clampdown on the opposition as a whole. Quite distinct from − and disowned by − the main national party PPP, (Pakistan Peoples' Party, led by Benazir Bhutto), Al-Zulfikar had reportedly fallen apart by 1984, torn apart by failure and internal rivalries.

A theory of Indian government involvement in a plot to get rid of the General is scarcely credible. Even if India's Prime Minister Rajiv Gandhi has frequently complained of Pakistan aiding and training Sikh terrorists, India is highly unlikely to have resorted to such a plot. Certainly, Zia's death has not removed the underlying rivalry and mutual suspicion which persists between the two states.

The General's sudden removal exposed the underlying instability of Pakistan. In spite of assurances that elections would go ahead, there was inevitably great uncertainty about the elections due in November. There was scepticism in some political circles as to what role the dominant armed forces would allow politicians to take in the government. It was claimed by some − holding to the common Pakistani belief that ultimately the USA pulls all the strings in Pakistan − that the Americans would never "permit" elections which might damage their special relationship with Pakistan.

There were also many optimists, though, who believed that the Military High Command did at last sincerely wish a democratically-elected government − of moderate tendency, at least − to succeed, and for it to take over responsibility from the interim administration.

ZIA THE MAN

General Zia-ul-Haq had lasted in power eleven years, longer than any of his predecessors, the series of Prime Ministers and Presidents since 1947. Underestimated and even ridiculed by some at first as a far from bright career army officer — and even as a comedian, a Pakistani version of the clowning film star Terry Thomas — Zia proved them all wrong.

He outwitted time and again the professional politicians ranged against military dictatorship in Pakistan. Indeed, by the end of his long career some observers saw Zia less as a military dictator than an astute politician, playing off the various rival forces which, if united, could have brought him down.

Claiming to lead a caretaker administration which would hold elections within ninety days, Zia enjoyed considerable public backing when he first took over at a time of great crisis in July 1977. The Pakistan People's Party government under Z.A. Bhutto had blatantly rigged elections, provoking fierce street fighting and a poisoned political atmosphere which threatened civil war. Activists of opposition parties, drawn from right and left of the political spectrum, were united in their determination to bring down Bhutto, who by 1977 had alienated even many of is early admirers.

In most respects, Zia was far from being a typical Pakistani military ruler. Zia was personally honest, modest and simple in his lifestyle, a devout and pious Muslim — a man obsessed by Islam, according to many Pakistani critics who believed that, not for the first time, the cloak of Islam was being cynically exploited to cover, and legitimise, what was really a crude dictatorship.

Undoubtedly, Zia's appetite for power grew with the exercise of power from 1977. He had a strong sense of mission, and a burning ambition to remould his country by introducing wide-ranging Islamic reforms.

PAKISTAN AFTER ZIA

The change might have considerable impact on Pakistan's foreign relations, as well as shaking up domestic politics. The major topics which this book will attempt to discuss in detail are outlined below.

Pakistan's policy towards Afghanistan, already unpopular with wide sections of the domestic public, has come immediately under greater pressure. A successor government is likely to suspend arms deliveries to Afghan guerrillas, as required under the Geneva accords.

Pakistan looks set to obey the accords to the letter, instead of continuing to further the private agreement between the Super Powers as to "symmetry" of arms to be supplied to their respective sides in this proxy war.

Relations with Iran and the conservative Arab states of the Gulf are too complex to expect immediate changes. Pakistan's important military presence in the Gulf states is likely to continue indefinitely. In spite of the peace hopes in the war between Iran and Iraq, the smaller Arab states are keen to retain a reliable and

6

efficient military back-up in the form of Pakistani advisers, instructors, skilled technicians and, in some cases, entire military units based in the Gulf region. Saudi Arabia and Pakistan became much closer during the 1980s. This degree of closeness looks unlikely to last. Under General Zia an Islamisation policy much favoured in Riyadh was pushed hard in Pakistan. Saudi funding played a big part in paying for arms for the Afghan mujahidin. On both scores, Pakistan's moving away from Saudi goals under a new civilian government could drive a wedge between them.

Long-standing difficulties with Pakistan's inveterate rival India are not likely to be resolved quickly. Hopes of reconciliation have been dashed many times before. Yet Zia's death could at last pave the way for a gradual lessening of hostility between the two neighbours, if a stable civilian government emerges.

China is regarded in Islamabad as Pakistan's oldest and most reliable ally. Chinese technical help has been important in building up Pakistani heavy industry – notably in armaments.

Since the Soviet invasion of Afghanistan at the end of 1979, the two governments have been united in their Afghan policy, of aiding the Afghan resistance so as to help defeat the Soviet-backed regime in Kabul. Chinese weapons played an essential part in the Afghan guerrilla resistance from its very beginnings.

China's main goal, getting an end to Soviet troops occupying bases in Afghanistan, may be achieved early in 1989, if the USSR keeps to the agreed schedule for withdrawal. China's close interest in Afghan developments may well decline sharply once Soviet troops have completed their withdrawal.

Zia's death could call into question the close links between Pakistan and the USA. The lavish tributes paid to the dead General by prominent US politicians show how this strategic relationship had become a personal one, and quite possibly over-dependent on Zia's continued good health.

Many Pakistanis are, with good reason, uneasy about the extent of Pakistan's cooperation in US strategic objectives in the wider Gulf region. Stories of secret treaties granting exclusive access to US military personnel in bases built in Pakistan's Baluchistan region are widely credited and bitterly resented.

However, the USA's special relationship with Pakistan carries some obvious benefits for both governments. US aid, divided about equally between military equipment and schemes for economic development, forms a large part of state revenue.

By the Reagan administration, Pakistan has been seen as a reliable friend, with military strength and proven efficiency, in a volatile strategic region. But this cosy relationship could come under strain by the actions of an influential lobby of US Senators in Washington. Renewed pressure on Pakistan to end its covert nuclear programme could soon result in sustained and eventually successful attempts to suspend US aid for Pakistan.

The crowds gathered at the funeral prayer meeting for the departed leader President (General) Zia-ul-Haq, in Islamabad.

Photo: Courtesy JANG, London

2
Pakistan: An Overview

Pakistan emerged in 1947 on the partition of British-ruled India. The new state was carved out of united India, with West Punjab, East Bengal combining with Sind, North West Frontier Province and Baluchistan. The northern one-third of Kashmir was absorbed later through armed intervention.

Pakistan consisted of two geographically separate parts, West Pakistan and East Pakistan, (known as Bangladesh since 1971). The capitals of the two wings of Pakistan were almost 1500 miles apart, and over 1,000 miles of Indian territory lay between the two wings. This might not have mattered so much if relations had not been so strained between the two states.

Though West Pakistan had 85 per cent of the total territory of 365,000 square miles, 55 per cent of the total population (around 100 million in 1947) was in the eastern wing. Some of the acute problems which developed in Pakistan were due to the fact that political power lay in the western wing, along with a disproportionate share of economic benefits. Besides this, there were distinct cultural differences between the Bengalis and the politically dominant groups, especially the Punjabis, who composed most of the army.

Unlike India, Pakistan did not long have the guidance or prestige of a well respected national figure capable of imposing his stamp on the country. Two key politicians died early on. The founder of the new state, Mohammad Ali Jinnah, was a sick man who died in 1948. Jinnah's trusted assistant, and Pakistan's first Prime Minister, Liaqat Ali Khan, was assassinated in 1951. No other leaders of stature emerged to fill the gap.

The majority of the elite taking up top positions in the new state, as civil servants, army officers and professionals, were outsiders, Muslims from cities of India who had migrated to Pakistan only at the time of partition. Many of them were unacquainted with the basic realities of the undeveloped, largely agrarian societies which Pakistan was allotted.

As a political organisation, the Muslim League could hardly be compared with India's Congress Party, as developed under Gandhi's influence from the

9

early 1920s. The Muslim League had no organisational base and no tradition of collective leadership. It was Jinnah himself who embodied the League in his person. In one instance, he is quoted as saying — ''What is Muslim League? — Myself, my sister and my typewriter!'' In most areas of Pakistan, the Muslim League had no grassroots backing as a political party, depending on cooperation from landlords for votes. This, of course, left the field wide open to other rival parties which developed after 1947.

The place of religion in the state was a vexed issue from the very beginning. Pakistan was certainly intended to be a state for the Indian Muslims, and the Sikhs and many Hindus left for India. However, the new state still contained a large minority of Hindu citizens, besides Christians and Parsees. Some forty million Muslims had remained in India — in some circles crudely thought of as hostages for the fair treatment of non-Muslims in Pakistan.

The precise place of Islam in the new state was bitterly disputed from 1948. Mullahs and puritanical Muslim activists led agitations to assert the primacy of Islam, as against secular minded politicians and a western-educated elite. The crucial question for Pakistan was the interpretation of Islam; modernist or backward-looking.

The Jamaat-i-Islami, an extreme right-wing Fundamentalist Muslim grouping influential in the cities, was active together with the newly-formed Jamiat-ul-Ulema-e-Islam, in demands for a 'purely Islamic' constitution. The religious lobby ardently wished Pakistan to be an 'ideological state' different from all others, and to become the testing ground for Islamic principles.[1]

The religious backlash was only one cause of great delay and huge controversy over the drafting of a Constitution for the new state. It proved highly damaging to the administration. Cases of corruption also marred the reputation of the government.

BENGALI GRIEVANCES

Many Bengali politicians of East Pakistan felt their wing was being exploited economically, and cheated of its due political weight. The question of fair and equitable representation for the two units by a federal type of government roused the passions of the politically conscious public in Eastern Bengal even as early as 1950.

An Interim Report of that year, which tried to concentrate power overmuch in the Executive based in the west, (in the then capital Karachi), sparked off street violence in East Pakistan, amid fury at what was felt to be ethnic discrimination. The planned changes were, for example, emotionally described in the free press as a 'shattering blow to East Bengal' aimed at holding it 'in bondage, political as well as economic', as well as an attempt to 'turn it virtually into a colony of West Pakistan, worse than that of Imperial Britain or France'.[2] The charge of flagrant economic exploitation became widely credited. The country's most important earner of foreign exchange by far was East Bengal's jute crop, which yielded over half of Pakistan's foreign earnings. Instead of being returned to East Pakistan, though, the great bulk of capital investment was regularly made in West Pakistan. Bengali nationalism and separatism developed as students and others active in politics expressed their grievances.

The eastern wing became a lucrative field of investment for mainly non-Bengali entrepreneurs and investors, favoured by state concessions. With its large population, the east formed a valuable captive market for manufactured goods imported from West Pakistan.

Another sensitive issue dividing east from west was the language issue. The primacy of English, Urdu and Bengali had their respective protagonists in Pakistan. The shooting down by police of Bengali language demonstrators in 1952 provoked renewed protests, and the formation of a United Front of opposition parties. Their demands were expressed in a programme of Twenty One Points, aptly described as, "the first charter of a disenfranchised middle class".[3] They aimed to achieve full equality between the provinces at federal level, and provincial autonomy for East Bengal.

When elections were held in East Pakistan in early 1954, the United Front won a landslide victory, leaving the 'ruling' Muslim League' just 11 seats out of the total 309 in the new Provincial Assembly. The victory was a hollow one, for the new Assembly was dissolved only two months later, and Governor's rule proclaimed for one year.

Outside the Punjab, the Muslim League did poorly in further elections, raising the fear in government circles in 1954 that a combination of Bengalis with Pathans and other non-Punjabis elected from areas in the western wing could get a majority in the national as well as federal assemblies, and oust them from power. The integration of the provinces in West Pakistan, by the One Unit scheme, followed directly from this perception.

THE MILITARY AND POLITICS

Parliamentary government gradually broke down in Pakistan, as crisis succeeded crisis. The way the failure of democracy in Pakistan was resolved had much to do with the close links existing between the army, the landlord class in the Punjab and the bureaucracy administering the state, (Civil Service of Pakistan, or CSP). These three powerful elements came from the same dominant semi-feudal class.

In the mid-1950s, as spineless, demoralised and disunited poiticians encountered serious difficulties in governing the country, both the bureaucracy and landowners welcomed the army's intervention. Their interests were, indeed, complementary. The civilian structure gradually coalesced around the army, leaving an illusion of democracy.

The first opportunity given the army to run the civil administration had come in the Punjab in 1953, at the time of organised riots against the Ahmadia community, a large Muslim sect hated by muslim bigots as heretics. Martial Law was imposed in Lahore from 6 March to 14 May 1953. The desperate law and order situation was quickly brought under control by Martial Law Administrators, who then proceeded to launch the 'Cleaner Lahore Campaign', a well-regarded attempt to improve health and sanitation conditions in what was by far the largest city of the Punjab.

This episode created a positive image of the army's efficiency and above all its ability to restore the peace when the civil administration had failed.[4] The army's rapid return to barracks also helped foster the idea that Pakistan's army was no Praetorian Guard, and that the Generals themselves had no political ambitions.

With the joint-military and bureaucratic regime which developed after Pakistan's first military coup in October 1958, Pakistan showed how easily and naturally these two key institutions inherited from the British Raj could combine. The regime of General/President Ayub Khan which followed was, in fact, essentially civilian in character.

A new system of 'Basic Democracy' was set up from 1959, aimed at bypassing the national political leadership. As a substitute for parliamentary democracy, it failed, nor did it succeed in its other purpose of legitimising the new regime. As President, Ayub was forced to abandon the attempt to organise a parliament without parties, himself becoming leader of one of the two factions into which the old Muslim League had broken up.

In a 1965 Presidential election, Ayub Khan was re-elected by almost two-thirds of the vote, against a united opposition candidate found in Miss Jinnah, the sister of Pakistan's founder. Significantly, though, Ayub Khan lost in the two major metropolitan cities of Karachi and Dacca. Strained relations with India and also Afghanistan made Pakistan's rulers and the public acutely conscious of security weaknesses. One key foreign relations issue on which there was substantial consensus in the early 1950s between all the major parties, the bureaucracy and the Military High Command was Pakistan's accepting US military aid and joining a US-sponsored regional military alliance. Pakistan joined SEATO and the Baghdad Pact, (later known as CENTO).

In 1955 General Ayub Khan publicly argued the merits of relying on the USA; he stated that Pakistan's defence and security needs made essential, "a strong and effective friend, whose interests should be to see that Pakistan remained a free country and was not subjugated by another country".[5]

Serious domestic problems also faced Pakistan's rulers from 1965 — though the Ayub Khan regime looked to many observers more solidly-based than previous governments. The head of the Awami League, Bengali politician H.S. Suhrawardy, was for a time the chief single opponent of President Ayub's regime. The National Awami Party, along with the communists and other left-wing forces in Pakistan, was badly divided, splitting into rival factions.

THE RISE OF CHAIRMAN BHUTTO

At the end of 1967, the stale atmosphere was broken. A former protege of Ayub Khan, ex- Foreign Minister and Sindhi landowner Zulfikhar Ali Bhutto launched a new party, Pakistan People's Party (PPP). It achieved a rapid and dramatic popularity in West Pakistan, particularly among students and the younger generation in general.

The PPP provided a focus against the unpopular dictatorship, and championed the cause of the deprived masses. He promised food, clothing, shelter and a share of power. In 1970, he went electioneering in a western style, to remote areas as well as the cities.

Through the PPP, Bhutto voiced the frustrations and aspirations of a wide part of the public, with mass appeal in Punjab and Sind, the two most important areas of the west. It exploited the prevalent anti-Indian sentiments, and the PPP chairman was an outspoken admirer of China, which he claimed was the firmest friend of Pakistan. However, the PPP really developed as an umbrella party, rather than one with a coherent ideology or shared goals.

In East Pakistan, the Awami League led by Sheikh Mujibur Rehman stood out as the spokesman of opposition to the regime. There followed five months of sustained student demonstrations and workers' strikes, virtually a mass rebellion in the cities of both East and West Pakistan, which finally brought down the Ayub regime in March 1969.

The second brief period of military rule which followed, under Yahya Khan, (1969-71), was a very turbulent one, which ended in the rout of the elite units of Pakistan's army, and the disintegration of the state.

The scale of the defeat suffered by Pakistan, traumatic for the nation, naturally proved deeply demoralising for the armed forces, paving the way for a further experiment with democracy, which began with promises of a brave new world. The brand of People's Party democracy under Z.A. Bhutto, though, was seriously flawed by its authoritarian tendency and harsh repression of political opposition.

It is now widely agreed that the dismemberment of Pakistan by the emergence of Bangladesh at the end of 1971 was tragic but, in all the circumstances, hardly surprising. Responsibility for this lay with a fatal combination of domestic and foreign factors.

There was the failure of General Yahya Khan, Z.A. Bhutto and Mujibur Rahman to compromise their respective positions and reach a political settlement yielding greater autonomy, before India's armed intervention in the eastern wing. A substantial number of well-informed Pakistanis allot much of the blame for the inability to reach a compromise to the intransigeance of Z.A. Bhutto, who backed the Yahya regime's actions in Bengal, and who, as a keen rival of Mujibur Rehman and a chauvinist politician to boot, stridently insisted on taking a hard line against the Bengali leader's six points.

BHUTTO IN POWER

In December 1971, after the military defeat, it was Bhutto to whom the Generals turned, almost inevitably. "The only hope was Bhutto who was literally the sole claimant to power", judged the editor (and onetime friend of Bhutto) Altaf Gauhar.[6]

Bhutto, who had returned to Islamabad from making his dramatic, emotional speeches arguing against partition before the United Nations in New York, was sworn in as president, at once exercising full martial law powers.

Bhutto's early actions won praise and even admiration. He restored the shattered morale of the nation, and brought back a parliamentary system of democracy. But with martial law still in force, he found it increasingly convenient simply to issue controversial laws by decree, ignoring the elected parliament, and avoiding the fuss and uncertainty of the democratic process.

Bhutto enjoyed mass appeal which seemed akin to geuine charisma. There were many Socialist slogans and a series of nationalisations, but expectations of real change, let alone a social or economic revolution, were gradually shown up to be wrongly-based.

Bhutto's early overwhelming popular support waned after his populist rhetoric became better appreciated. Fierce opposition was roused by Bhutto's authoritarian methods of keeping power, which included brutally-run concentration camps set up in Azad Kashmir, Sind and elsewhere. Bhutto ran the party — arguably the entire country, too — like his own large estate in Sind. Gangsterism and abuse of patronage took place on a larger scale than ever before.

"The whole edifice of the political system", claims the Pakistani analyst Hasan-Askari Rizvi, "was built around his personality".[7]

Bhutto was a complex and contradictory figure, highy intelligent and well educated, probably idealistic too, in the early years at least of his tenure of power. Bhutto's tragedy — and that of Pakistan too — was that in power he failed to control his natural arrogance and instinct for domination. He muzzled the press by tightly controlling the most influential media. He dismissed or imprisoned independent-minded politicians, journalists and editors, ignoring alike parliament and the admirable new Constitution which he had himself (ironically) introduced.

The PPP government was quite unable to solve the country's pressing economic problems, which it had actually aggravated by gross mismanagement. Its policies of nationalisation alienated the class of entrepreneurial investors, leading to a flight of capital from Pakistan. A programme of social reform had likewise alienated influential sections of the traditional elites of the country. Finally, Bhutto resorted to issuing decrees against sale of alcohol, together with a range of "Islamic reforms", which, however, failed to appease the Islamic elements in the opposition.

A five-year long guerrilla war in Baluchistan did great damage to the progressive image of the government, besides proving very difficult to win, even with an army of 100,000 men and huge destruction.

The Baluch adventure has been assessed by the Pakistani writer and political activist Tariq Ali as a disaster on every count; "Bhutto's downfall and the end of civilian rule can be traced directly to the PPP's refusal to tolerate a meaningful regional autonomy, or accept the principle of power-sharing within a federal framework."[8]

A strong coalition of heterogeneous opposition parties developed, devoted to bringing down Bhutto. Uniting as the Pakistan National Alliance (PNA), it was composed of nine parties; right-wing religious parties, notably Jamaat-i-Islami, Tehrik-i-Istiqlal and the National Democratic Party. It was led by some very determined politicians of the calibre of the Pathan nationalist Abdul Wali Khan.

Bhutto's blatant rigging of the March 1977 general elections — the first to be held since 1970 — infuriated wider sections of the public than had been drawn in during previous agitations. The elections took place against a background of class and ethnic conflict.

The PPP resorted to extensive rigging during the campaign and polling. In three out of four of Pakistan's four provinces, the provincial governments allegedly made vigorous efforts to recruit the entire bureaucracy – including police superintendants, deputy commissioners and the intelligence services – as party helpers. In many doubtful constituencies, polling staff were placed in fear of their lives by PPP thugs. In many parts of Pakistan, the "election" was in reality little other than a pretence of democracy. (The remarkable extent of the intimidation and deliberate rigging was documented in a three-volume white paper, published in 1978 by the military regime which succeeded to Bhutto).

The illegitimate tactics and cheating resorted to by the Bhutto government did much harm to the reputation of the PPP and, in the final analysis, were surely unworthy of the talented man who had claimed to wish to restore democracy, along with so many other promised benefits, to the people of Pakistan.

NOTES TO INTRODUCTION

1. see further, Wilfred Cantwell Smith, Pakistan as an Islamic State, Sh Muhammad Ashraf, Lahore, 1962; Freeland Abbott, Islam and Pakistan, Cornell, New York, 1968; Peter Hardy, The Muslims of British India, Cambridge U.P., 1972.
2. Inamur Rehman, Public Opinion and Political development in Pakistan, Oxford U.P., Karachi, 1982, p43.
3. Tariq Ali, Can Pakistan Survive? Penguin Books, Harmondsworth, 1983.
4. see Hasan-Askari Rizvi, The Military and Politics in Pakistan 1947-86, Progressive Publishers, Lahore, 1987, pp 60-62.
5. statement published in DAWN, Karachi, 18 January 1955.
6. Altaf Gauhar in The Guardian, London, 21 February 1979.
7. Hasan-Askari Rizvi, ibid, p 216, and see chapter 10 (The Turn of the Tide).
8. Tariq Ali, ibid, p 123.

3
A Flawed Democracy

Even the comparatively knowledgeable people in Pakistan in 1976 had hardly come across the name of Zia-ul-Haq when the then Prime Minister Zulfikar Ali Bhutto appointed him to the most coveted post of Chief of Staff of the Pakistan Army. That was 1st of March, 1976. Just after sixteen months into that appointment, General Zia deposed his mentor and benefactor and assumed power, which he perhaps secretly wished to keep till his death. And that he did, although he perhaps never envisaged that it would end that soon. People compared Zia with Franco of Spain, Salazar of Portugal and Emperor Haile Sellasie of Ethiopia. Before his abrupt departure from the scene, government-controlled newspapers in Pakistan were publishing articles comparing him with those long serving rulers. And one reporter even asked the General himself whether he wished to break the record of France in government. In reply, he simply said, 'No'. But the preparations were there. The National Assembly after the scheduled non-party elections in November 1988 would have consisted of individual members free of any party whip. They could have been bribed and cajoled and manoeuvred to side with him.

When Zia deposed Bhutto and took over in July 1977 no one, not even his fellow generals were prepared to give him more than a few months. When General Zia announced elections to be held within ninety days, many of his compatriots thought he would be lucky to survive even that long. Diplomats in Islamabad at the time used to joke about his moustache and teeth and a common joke among them was that the moustache was phoney and he used a new denture every day. They used to call him a clown, and in their reports back to their governments, most of the diplomats predicted that the General would be replaced by some other senior military man who looked more the part. He proved all of them wrong.

No one really knows why Bhutto chose General Zia for the post of Chief of Army Staff. Circles close to the late Mr Bhutto used to say that Bhutto was impressed by Zia-ul-Haq's simplicity and loyalty. They said that among the top

17

generals Zia was the only one who talked to the point, assumed no airs and gave an impression of total loyalty. There are, however, theories. Bhutto was himself a product of martial law. He nevertheless became a mass leader and changed the course of Pakistan politics but his political career began under martial law and ended under martial law. He became a government minister when General Iskander Mirza took over in 1958. After the ignominious exit of Iskander Mirza, Bhutto continued with General Ayub Khan. Under Ayub Khan in his system of limited democracy, Bhutto for a time was the Secretary General of Ayub Khan's ruling party the Muslim League.

Bhutto had seen how General Yahya Khan, the Commander-in-Chief of the Pakistan Army, forced President Ayub Khan to step down and hand over the reigns of power to him in March 1969. The political movement against the Ayub government, led by Mr Bhutto himself, was continuing when General Yahya Khan decided that his time had come and he, along with the chiefs of the air force and navy drove to the President's House and demanded Ayub Khan's resignation. Without any hesitation and without any resistance whatsoever Ayub Khan complied. Bhutto also knew that after the debacle of East Pakistan it was the generals of the demoralised and shaken army of Pakistan who invited him to come and take over. Bhutto knew that power was the gift of the generals. That was why when he responded to the general's invitation and reached Islamabad on the 20th of December 1971 and when General Yahya Khan asked him to assume leadership he insisted on being appointed the Chief Martial Law Administrator, perhaps the first civilian chief martial law administrator in recent history.

Mr Bhutto arrived at Chaklala airport from the United States. A huge crowd was at the airport to greet him because not only the generals but millions of ordinary people in Pakistan believed at the time that he was the only saviour, the last hope for the dismembered country and demoralised people. Bhutto said he had come back to pick up the pieces. The people followed him from the airport to the Presidents' House. There was no official word for a long time. There were, however, leaks about a heated argument going on inside. An argument about what? One waiting journalist jokingly suggested that Bhutto wanted to be the Chief Martial Law Administrator, and the generals were resisting. A while later the joke turned out to be true. The official word came; Bhutto was Chief Martial Law Administrator and also the President. General Yahya Khan could not envisage a civilian to be the chief of the armed forces, first he insisted on retaining the office of Chief Martial Law Administrator, but later was willing to hand it over to his loyal lieutenant, General Abdul Hamid

Khan. Bhutto, however, absolutely insisted. Perhaps that the only time in Pakistan history when the generals had no options. They had to concede.

The other time, though in different circumstances, was when Bhutto dismissed General Gul Hassan whom he himself had appointed as Commander-in-Chief of the Pakistan Army. But the manner in which General Gul Hassan was dismissed showed vividly how seriously Bhutto took the army. The wounds of the dismemberment of the country from the bloody civil war in the eastern half, and the Pakistan Army's defeat at the hands of the Indian armed forces were very fresh. The Pakistan Army had not yet been able to shrug off the sense of humiliation and shame, and Bhutto was still riding the wave of overwhelming popular support. He was at one and the same time Chief Martial Law Administrator, President and Commander-in-Chief of the Pakistan Army.

Yet even then General Gul Hasan, the Chief of Army Staff, could not be dismissed in a routine manner. Ghulam Mustafa Khar, the Governor of Punjab and Bhutto's closest aide at the time, was summoned to Rawalpindi and asked to take General Gul Hassan and Air Marshal Rahim to Lahore. Mr Khar is reported to have told Gul Hassan and Rahim that the President was addressing an important meeting in Lahore and wanted them to be present. Unsuspectingly they both joined the Governor in his official car. Amazingly for Pakistan, the Governor himself was at the wheel, dispensing with his official driver. When they were midway between Rawalpindi and Lahore, Bhutto made the official announcement of the dismissal of General Gul Hassan and Air Marshal Rahim. They only learned of their fate when they were safely confined, incommunicado, in the Government House in Lahore. Bhutto got to know very well, of course, the powers of the Pakistan Generals. He knew and fully appreciated that he could come to power only with the support and approval of the military – and that if he hoped to keep power, then he must establish a firm relationship with key Generals.

General Zia's character and background may well have helped convince Bhutto that through Zia he could best hope to keep in with the military. The forceful Prime Minister may well have been struck by Zia's modesty and efficiency, but it is more likely that the quality of personal loyalty was what he was searching for.

ZIA THE MAN

Zia-ul-Haq was born on 12 August 1924 in Jullundur, in the eastern part of the Punjab. His father was a clerk in the Army General Headquarters in Delhi, and he moved to Delhi along with his family in 1930. Zia was educated in Delhi, receiving his early religious education from a well-known figure, Moulvi Vali Mohammad who is still alive. Moulvi Vali Mohammad used to lead prayers in the local mosque. Zia got his higher education at St. Stephens College, a prestigious educational institution run by Christian missionaries. He received his army commission in May 1945. Zia's cavalry regiment was sent to Burma in the closing months of the Second World War, and he was sent to Malaya and Java as well during that time, but is not reported to have been involved in action.

After partition of the subcontinent, he opted for Pakistan and in 1955 graduated from the Staff College Quetta. In 1963, he attended the United States Command and General Staff College, and on his return to Pakistan was appointed instructor at the Command and Staff College, Quetta, and promoted to the rank of Lt. Col. Zia stayed in Quetta instructing young officers in the techniques of fighting and command. He was promoted to the rank of Brigadier in 1969, and Major General three years later. As a Major General he commanded an armoured division. He rose to the rank of a Lt. General in April 1975, and was appointed a corps commander. Zia was based in Multan Punjab, and it was there that he first met Bhutto, the then Prime Minister, and offered him a copy of the holy book as a token of his obedience. In less than eleven months, on March 1, 1976, he was promoted to the rank of full General, and appointed Chief of Staff of the Pakistan Army. At the time there were at least eight other senior Lt. Generals aspiring for the coveted post.

As a devout Muslim, General Zia offered his prayers five times a day and bore its mark on his forehead − the 'Gutta' − which appears on the forehead of all those who offer prayers regularly because the forehead is put on the ground so frequently. In fact General Zia came from that batch of Pakistan military officers who can be described as post-1965 cadre. Pakistan's Army was early on led by British trained, Sandhurst educated officers. They normally followed the ways of the Raj. General Ayub Khan, the first Pakistan Commander-in-Chief, never had his dinner without having a couple of whiskies. The second Pakistani Commander-in-Chief General Yahya Khan was a heavy drinker who before taking over from Ayub Khan was a regular visitor to the Pindi Club, the most famous club for the British officers of the Northern command under the Raj. After independence as the Army headquarters was at Rawalpindi it retained its importance. Most of the Army officers had their gin and tonics there, before going home for lunch, as well as their whisky and soda before dinner. Yahya Khan visited the club regularly, and quite often there were boozing sessions.

The atmosphere is reflected in a joke current in Rawalpindi at the time when

A FLAWED DEMOCRACY

General Yahya Khan became the Commander-in-Chief of the Pakistan Army. In the early hours of one morning after one of these boozing sessions, General Yahya Khan came out to the portice of the club to go home when he noticed a nearby tree which he thought was not straight. He became annoyed. "Why is the tree not straight?" One of the friends suggested pushing it to make it straight. All of them rolled up their sleeves and started pushing the tree to make it straight — to the amazement of the few bearers who were still awake. They kept on pushing the tree for quite a long time when one of them got a bit sober and said, "Sir, the mission is accomplished'. The General looked approvingly at the tree and boarded his car.

General Yahya Khan, however, belonged to an older generation of military officers who followed the British ways of military and social life. Those not trained in that manner usually followed the example of their senior officers. It all changed dramatically after the 1965 war. It was the same with all these clubs, the Pindi and Peshawar clubs, the Lahore and Karachi Gymkhanas and the Army mess in Dacca and Chittagong. Before 1965 they had always been full of young (and not so young) officers drinking whisky or gin or beer. The clubs all became more or less deserted after the '65 war. Quite a few officers, after perhaps looking death in the face during the war, gave up alcohol.

General Zia was never among them, though he was in the same age-group. Zia returned home to his wife and family, instead of going to the club. He was reputed to be a non-drinker who never touched alcohol. He used to smoke at one time, but even gave up cigarettes after 1977. In one of his appeals to the nation he had asked the people to give up pan (betel leaves). They were expensive because betel is imported from Bangladesh. Zia was then taunted by the pan-chewing opposition leader, Maulana Shah Ahmad Noorani, as to why the President did not himself give up smoking. And he did give it up.

Why Zia-ul-Haq? Bhutto could have found other officers in the Pakistan Army who would be totally loyal and trustworthy. There are many theories about the choice, Bhutto had first met Zia-ul-Haq in Multan in 1975. Zia was the general Officer Commanding. The then governor of Punjab, Sadiq Hussain Qureshi, had invited the Prime Minister to his ancestral home there. The story goes that Zia came early and asked Qureshi to provide him with a copy of the holy Koran. Qureshi obliged. When Bhutto arrived and Zia was introduced to him, he made a 'humble request' to the Prime Minister to accept the copy of the holy book, as on that holy book he used to pray every morning and evening for the lasting rule of Bhutto which had given the people of Pakistan, so Zia said, a hope for the future.

General Zia, unlike other high ranking military officers, never addressed the

Prime Minister as 'Mr Prime Minister'. According to General Zia's own account, he always addressed Bhutto as 'sir' — even after deposing him in 1977. While in the presence of Bhutto, Zia never failed to mention that he was a simple soldier, and his duty was merely to obey orders. There is a story that when General Zia achieved his ambition and was promoted Chief of Army Staff, once being called in directly to the Prime Minister's office, Zia put the cigarette he was smoking into his pocket — still burning! and entered.

When the announcement of Zia-ul-Haq's promotion to the rank of General and Chief of Army Staff came, it sank in slowly. After a few days an American diplomat in Islamabad who knew Urdu told a group of journalists that Bhutto had got another Nura. It was an interesting observation. Nura — Noor Mohamad — was Mr Bhutto's personal servant. Bhutto liked him as many masters like devoted servants. Noora accompanied Bhutto on almost every visit abroad. He used to sit in the economy class of the plane, and was always addressed very respectfully, not like a servant at all, as Noora Saheb — not only by journalists, but by the all-powerful secretaries of the Pakistan government. Some of them genuinely believed that Noora was a confidante of the Prime Minister, and that a word from him might be very helpful to their career. On several occasions even the all powerful secretaries of the government were seen approaching Noora to know whether it was right to see the Prime Minister over a particular problem.

WHY ZIA?

The "Muslim Brotherhood" link is one of the most intriguing theories to explain why Zia may have been chosen by Bhutto. It rests, though, on pure speculation.

General Zia was close to Pakistan's main Muslim fundamentalist organisation, the Jamaat-i-Islami, which Bhutto wanted to contain. The Jamaat-i-Islami had never been a popular political party in the subcontinent. The first time the Jamaat got representation in Pakistan's National Assembly was in the 1970 elections, and then too only four of its members could get elected out of 146 in the then West Pakistan. The Jamaat never gained popular support, nevertheless it had much influence in the Pakistan Army. That was sensed much earlier by Field Marshal Ayub Khan — General Ayub Khan after assuming power, had promoted himself to the rank of Field Marshal. It was Ayub Khan's government which banned the Jamaat-i-Islami in the early sixties. The Jamaat was banned by a government decree. Its leader Maulana Abul Ala Moudoodi had been sentenced to death during earlier Martial law in 1953. The death sentence was not carried out, as the king of Saudi Arabia reportedly threatened to sever diplomatic relations with Pakistan if the Pakistan government went ahead with the Maulana's execution. The Maulana's life was saved, and the Jammat is still politically very active in Pakistan.

It was by far the most staunch ally of General Zia, at least in the early years of his government. Maulana Abul Ala Moudoodi had retured from active politics due to his failing health, and Maulana Tufail Mohammad was the chief of the Jammat when General Zia took over. He was said to be related to Zia. Although none of them revealed the true nature of the relationship, but after Zia's take over people used to talk of 'Mamoon Bhanjey ka khel' – that it was a game of maternal uncle and his nephew (Maulana Tufail Mohammad was said to be a maternal uncle of Zia).

The Jamaat-i-Islami is a secretive organisation organised in cadres, and run more or less like communist parties in the Third world countries. It has a large band of sympathisers, some active, some latent. The active sympathisers are supposed to come out on the street at the call of their leaders, while the latent ones support the Jamaat financially or otherwise. Membership of the Jamaat is controlled. Only tried and tested sympathisers are allowed membership of the party. Although no direct connection has been proved between the two, the Jamaat is believed to be akin to Akhwan-ul-Muslemeen, the militant Muslim organisation of Egypt. The Saudi Arabian government, wholeheartedly supports the Jamaat-i-Islami in Pakistan through generous funding.

The Jamaat has been regarded as a potential threat by every Pakistani government since the days of Ayub Khan. Its importance as a potential threat was once again revealed when in early 1977 Bhutto, faced with the country-wide agitation against the rigging in the general elections, went to Lahore to see the ailing Maulana Abul Ala Maudoodi whose party, the Jamaat-i-Islami was in the forefront of that agitation. He did not care to go to any other leader.

Another theory for the coup is that of the ''hidden hand'' – that of the USA. Bhutto's pursuit of the so-called ''Islamic bomb'' had caused a rupture with the USA. The total blocking of US aid to Pakistan, together with heavy-handed US pressure on France to abandon its collaboration with Pakistan in the nuclear field, increased existing pressures on the ailing government. Bhutto later recorded, in a much-quoted remark, that the US Secretary of State Henry Kissinger bluntly warned him in August 1976, ''we can destabilize your government and make a horrible example out of you''.

Washington's attempts to thwart Pakistan's nuclear ambitions naturally generated great resentment against the USA. Bhutto exploited this sentiment for all it was worth in the final period of his power. On 21 April 1977, in the wake of violent protest demonstrations against the elections, martial law had been declared in three major cities – Karachi, Lahore and Hyderabad. In

23

emotional speeches in Parliament and outside, Bhutto claimed that the disturbances in the country were the machinations of the CIA, and that an international conspiracy was afoot to bring him down. The menace of the CIA was deliberately exaggerated into an explanation for the mass protests which threatened his rule.

In April 1977, the Prime Minister suddenly came to Rajah Bazar, a middle class shopping centre in Rawalpindi, and, standing up in an open jeep, delivered an impromptu harangue to the startled onlookers. During his emotional speech, Bhutto took out a piece of paper from his pocket and, waving it to the assembled audience, declared that this was a letter from America which gave categorical proof that the USA was behind the agitation.

Many PPP supporters still believe that the USA was behind the upsurge of protests against the PPP government in 1977. Probably most Pakistanis believe that the military coup which followed was approved by, or even planned by the Americans. That the protests were rooted in domestic politics cannot be doubted, though, by objective observers. They were funded by popular fury against Bhutto's abuse of power, not by CIA dollars.

US involvement or prior approval of the coup of 5 July 1977 is certainly highly likely, though actual evidence for this is murky. There are some well-founded reports, though, that General Zia and other senior army officers consulted with the US ambassador to Pakistan shortly before taking the decision to intervene. That the generals would have actually needed help from the CIA or any other US agency in planning or executing the coup seems far more dubious. It also flies in the face of the experience of many other Third World countries where the military has assumed a dominant position.

4
Operation Fair Play

Zulfikar Ali Bhutto called the elections on February 7, 1977. He acted according to the constitution which had been unanimously passed by the National Assembly in 1973, but gave the minimum days required for the preparation. The main opposition party, the National Awami Party was demoralised. Its leaders, including Khan Wali Khan, were being tried for sedition. Its ally, the Jamiat-ul-Islam was only partially active in the provinces of North West Frontier and Baluchistan. The Muslim League was a house divided in itself. Jamiat-ul-Ulema-Islam or JUP of Maualana Shah Ahmad Noorani had not been able to extend its constituency from a section of Mohajirs (refugees who migrated from India after the partition and settled in Pakistan) in some cities in the province of Sind. Only the Jamaat-i-Islami was active with its small but dedicated band of workers. But it was bitterly opposed by its traditional rivals, the JUI and the JUP. The Tehrik-i-Istiqlal of retired air marshal Asghar Khan was yet to take off. Bhutto perhaps thought that the dividend opposition would not be able to unite under the circumstances and his People's Party would sweep the polls.

However, the usually divided opposition sprang a surprise and within a matter of days formed a united front, in the name of Pakistan National Alliance. They chose the Pir of Pagara as their leader. He is the hereditary chief of the Hur tribe in the province of Sind which, under the leadership of the father of the present Pir, fought against the British. The Pir of Pagara had never been active in Pakistan politics. His main hobbies had been Shikar, (hunting) horse racing and kite flying, but he rose to the occasion and proved a formidable opponent to Zulfikar Ali Bhutto. They both belonged to the province of Sind, and both of them were big landlords. But the Pir of Pagara had an added advantage. he was the chief of a large tribe fanatically devoted to him.

Within no time the Pakistan National Alliance became a force to reckon with, and put up a strong fight against the People's Party in the elections. The elections were rigged. Bhutto had perhaps failed to realise that five years of his government had alienated him from the middle class urban population. Merchants and traders

25

were fed up with his policies of nationalisation and trade restrictions. His Federal Security Force under the highly discredited bureaucrat, Masood Mahmood, had become a force of oppression in the cities. Many of his People's Party workers had become corrupt, and the common people were scared of the gangsters among them. Mullahs, whether they belonged to the Jamaat-i-Islami or the JUI or the JUP, had always been after his blood. His brand of socialism had turned the students and the youth against his party. When he came out on the streets against Ayub Khan, the students were in the vanguard of the anti-Ayub Khan movement. The very first martyr of that movement was a nineteen year old Abdul Hameed, a student of Rawalpindi Polytechnic. He was with a large group of students going to receive Mr Bhutto, who was that day coming from Peshawar to Rawalpindi by car. The students wanted to take him to the city in a procession. The police opened fire and Abdul Hameed was killed. When Ayub Khan was in power, all the major student unions in colleges and universities were dominated by left wing pro-Bhutto elements. After Bhutto took over, the situation had gradually been reversed. It was the Jamiat-i-Tulba, the student wing of the Jamaat-i-Islami, which dominated the student unions.

Bhutto also lacked political wisdom, or perhaps his cronies and sycophants had given him the impression that he was the undisputed leader of the country, as was Chairman Mao in China. In the 1970 elections, he had contested in five constituencies and had got elected from four. In the 1977 elections, he filed his nomination papers in his home constituency of Larkana. A leader of the Jamaat-i-Islami, Maulana Jan Mohammed Abbasi, wanted to oppose him. It was common knowledge that no one, not even the strongest of his opponents, could defeat Bhutto in his home constituency. Poor Maulana Jan Mohammad Abbasi was not even a strong opponent. If allowed to contest he would certainly have lost his security deposit. But he was not even allowed to file his nomination papers. So there was no opposing candidate and Bhutto was declared elected 'unopposed'. The respected English language newspaper of Karachi, Dawn, published a four column photograph of Bhutto the next day with the caption, 'the undisputed leader'. That showed the shape of things to come.

Government functionaries, the deputy commissioners, the police superintendants, the tehsildars, all were directed to see that the People's Party candidates won. As are the ways of civil servants and bureaucrats, perhaps they showed more enthusiasm then they were supposed to. Many of the opposition leaders now agree that even if there had been no rigging, the People's Party would have won the 1977 elections. The opposition was only active in the cities of the provinces of Punjab and Sind, and it was very likely that a majority of

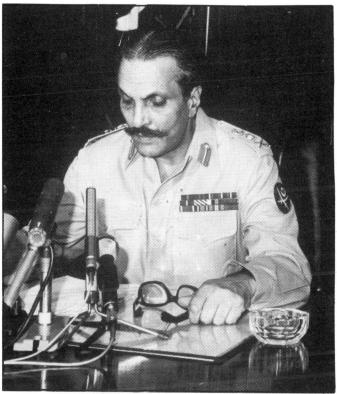

General Zia-ul-Haq broadcasting to the nation, and the world, his motives for military takeover and his plans for future of Pakistan, on July 5, 1977.

Photo: Courtesy of JANG London

the voters in the provinces of North West Frontier and Baluchistan would have gone against the People's Party, because of its treatment of the majority parties in those two provinces, the National Awami Party and the Jamiat-ul-Ulema-i-Islam. The People's Party had never been popular in those two provinces, and had further alienated itself from the people by the way the coalition government of the National Awami Party and the JUL in the two provinces were dismissed.

Thus the People's Party was very likely to be defeated in Baluchistan and the North West Frontier, and quite likely also in the cities in Punjab and Sind. But the provinces of Baluchistan and the North West Frontier had few seats in the National Assembly, and the majority of voters in Punjab and Sind were in the rural areas. They were traditionally controlled by landlords, and the majority of landlords was aligned with the ruling People's Party. The elections were nevertheless rigged in favour of the ruling party, and the furore it started gave the chance to the Army to seize power again.

The opposition Pakistan National Alliance gave a call to boycott the provincial elections due to be held two days later, and in cities, at least, the boycott was almost total. Then started the Pakistan National Alliance movement called 'the movement for Nizam-i-Mustafa' − the system followed by the Prophet Muhammad, a political system based on Islamic principles. That movement very soon developed into a formidable force with such strange bedfellows as the mullahs of the Jamaat-i-Islami, the JUI and the JUB, secular workers of the National Awami Party and the Qoumi Mahaz-i-Azadi and the liberal centrists of the Muslim League and the Tehrik-i-Istiqlal. It is now widely believed that the movement for Nizam-i-Mustafa was not in fact a movement for Islam, it was a movement for political change. Bhutto failed to realise that as well. Instead of giving concessions to the people and trying to win them over, he tried to contain the mullahs. He unwisely tried to fight them on their chosen ground for which he or his party were neither prepared nor qualified. He declared the Ahmadis non-Muslims. Ahmadis (also known as Qadianis) are a small but powerful sect and had been ardent supporters of Bhutto, as the fundamentalist mullahs wanted to cast them out of the Muslim fold, and Bhutto was seen as secular, liberal and anti-mullah. To contain the mullahs, Bhutto also banned alcohol and horse racing, although during the same period he provocatively declared in an open air meeting that he used to drink alcohol. The movement was not contained, and it rapidly spread. Bhutto had already used the army in Baluchistan, now he had to use it again and then in Punjab. The Pakistan Army is mostly a Punjabi army and it was difficult for the Punjabi soldier to shoot at his own kith and kin. General Iqbal, the then General Officer Commanding of Lahore, publicly expressed his indignation.

Bhutto was forced to release the leaders of the Pakistan National Alliance who had earlier been detained and to start talks with them. The Prime Minister was obliged to admit publicly that there had been rigging, but claimed it had been only in some thirty constituencies. The opposition disagreed and demanded fresh elections. There was a spokesman from each side to brief the media at the end of every session. The People's Party spokesman was Maulana Kausar Niazi, Bhutto's minister for religious affairs, and the opposition spokesman was professor Ghafoor Ahmad, a leader of the Jamaat-i-Islami. Both of them, Maulana Kausar Niazi as well as professor Ghafoor Ahmad, have written full accounts of those talks. Both of them agree that an agreement had been reached between the two. Also involved closely were the Secretary General of the Defence Ministry, Mr Ghulam Ishaque Khan, and the Chief of Army Staff, General Zia. Several journalists were telephoned every evening by aides of the two to find out what was happening. Bhutto was perhaps made aware of their concern, for he invited General Zia to one of the sessions. Ostensibly Zia attended the session to brief the opposition leaders of the possible threat to Pakistan's security, but the main purpose, as is now known, was to have a sense of the state of negotiations.

Far from breaking down, the negotiations in fact succeeded, and an agreement was reached. The People's Party agreed that there had been rigging in the elections. The opposition, for its part, agreed that there was no need for fresh elections to all the National Assembly seats. They agreed that there should be fresh elections in eighty National Assembly constituencies, but fresh elections for all the provincial assemblies, since the opposition had boycotted them. It was also agreed that the elections would be held within ninety days.

The agreement was to be signed after the central committee of the opposition Pakistan National Alliance had approved it. The draft of the agreement was discussed in the central committee meeting of the Pakistan National Alliance and it met with approval from most of the members. They were happy, rather jubilant that they had forced Bhutto to bow down to their demand. They believed that once the all-powerful People's Party was in retreat, and seeing the mood of the country after a successful movement spearheaded by the Pakistan National Alliance, they would win a majority of the eighty National Assembly seats to be contested, and would surely have a fair share in the provincial assemblies which were to be elected afresh.

However, there were some who were not happy. The Pakistan National Alliance was dominated by three parties — the Muslim League, the National Awami Party and the Jamaat-i-Islami. They would have been the major beneficiaries and they were keen for the agreement. The Jamiat-ul-Ulema-i-Islam of Maulana Mufti Mahmood and the Jamiat-ul-Ulema-i-Pakistan of Maulana Shah Ahmad Noorani were reported to have gone along with the majority opinion. They had their solid political constituencies, and did not stand to lose. But another opposition politician, Air Marshal Asghar Kan of the Tehrik-i-Istiqlal was reported to have refused. While in captivity Asghar Khan, it was claimed, had written to the Chiefs of Staff of the Army, Navy and Air Force to intervene and save the nation from further bloodshed. Asghar Khan argued that Bhutto could not be trusted at all, so there should be no agreement with him.

Since the Alliance worked on consensus, there was no majority decision. The central committee of the Alliance, therefore, did not approve the compromise. The agreement was not signed, sealed and delivered. The Pakistan National Alliance is no longer alive, but many leaders of its component parties now publicly admit that had they signed the agreement, they could perhaps have saved Pakistan from eleven years of military and semi-military rule and the uncertain political future that the country is facing now. Perhaps they are right. It wold have been very difficult for the generals to strike when almost all the political forces of the country were united on a political future for the country.

General Zia's operation Fair Play — operation foulplay to many — was, of course, not planned overnight. General Zia was busy planning his political manoeuvre over the months of crisis. The Rawalpindi Corps commander, Lt. Gen. Faiz Ali Chishti was said to have been his closest aide in the conspiracy. There are some who suggest they were even instrumental in making the Pakistan National Alliance central committee fail to sign the agreement with the People's Party. If the agreement had been signed, it would have been very difficult to find another pretext; if they had intervened at that stage, it would have been an action against all the viable political forces of the country.

In the event the operation Fair Play went ahead smoothly, precisely. As the clock struck midnight, the guard at the Prime Minister's house was changed. All those who had been on guard were removed and soldiers from a regiment of Lt. Gen. Chishti's corps were posted at the Prime Ministers' house.

The movements of the guards were noticed and some one told the Prime Minister that there were some suspicious movements going on. He reportedly did not believe it. How could his protege General Zia do such a thing to him? He had to believe it, though, when an army officer came in and, without saluting him, said that the Army had taken over. Bhutto tried to telephone Zia. The telephone lines had been disconnected. Later, on his special request he was connected to General Zia who reportedly told Bhutto that he was sorry, but had been forced to perform that unpleasant task, and that Bhutto along with other political leaders of both the ruling and opposition parties would be taken into what he called 'protective custody'. Then the telephone again went dead. Nobody was allowed to leave or enter the house, and Bhutto with members of his family sat outside in the lawns of the house which had seen people like Ayub Khan and Yahya Khan go unsung, unwept and uncried for, assuring his daughter Benazir that there was nothing to worry about and everything would be alright.

In the early hours of 5 July 1977, Bhutto was sent to Murree and lodged in a rest house. General Zia made his announcement that the army had to take that unpleasant duty to save the country from imminent civil war and bloodshed, and pledged that elections would be held within ninety days in October, when power would be returned to civilian rulers (see Appendix A). It was not only Bhutto who did not believe it. There were many in the opposition parties who believed the imposition of martial law to be an act of collusion between Bhutto and General Zia, so that the opposition could be crushed by the army and Bhutto could return as a hero after the October 1977 elections, the army having done the dirty work. Many opposition politicians indeed believed it was a 'Noora Kushti' − a wrestling bout in which the opponents agree beforehand who would be allowed to win.

In opposition circles, it was thought that the agreement that Bhutto had agreed to sign with the opposition Pakistan National Alliance was only to gain time, and that Bhutto had had second thoughts. He wanted to be the undisputed leader and was not prepared to have a strong opposition in the National Assembly, nor to see the provinces of the North West Frontier and Baluchistan ruled by opposition parties.

The way the government of Baluchistan was dismissed and the government of the North West Frontier forced to resign, the way Khan Wali Khan and other leaders of his National Awami Party were arrested and tried for sedition was fresh in people's memory. They did not believe that a man of Bhutto's cleverness could be outmanoeuvred by his own protege − and that too a man who looked to some no better than a clown.

General Zia soon visited Bhutto in the government rest house at Murree, accompanied by Lt. Gen. Chishti. And reportedly during that meeting Bhutto lost his temper and abused Zia for what he had done. One théory was that that outburst was the real cause of Zia's later actions. Some even say it was General Chishti who believed himself to be the real power behind Zia, and forced General Zia to seize power at this stage. That is hard to believe. General Zia always gave the impression that he was a reluctant ruler. He said he was a simple soldier and his place was in the barracks, not in the Presidents' House. But every military dictator says so. It is hard to believe that there are some who are convinced. General Zia knew very well that in Pakistan only the army chief had the power. There had been no political organisation in Pakistan − and there are none even today − which could mobilise the masses against the army.

ROTI, KAPRA AUR MAKAN

Bhutto had promosed abolition of zamindari, the system of land ownership introduced by the British in the early stages of the Raj in India, he had promised nationalisation of big industries, banks and insurance companies, fundamental

31

rights and 'roti, kapra and makan' (bread, clothes and a house) to the poor.

Under his government banks and insurance companies and some industries were nationalised and a sort of land reform carried out, still, however, leaving thousands of acres in the hands of individual owners, the big landlords. Nationalisation of Pakistan's industries though proved a fiasco, since instead of being run by the experts of that particular field they were then run by civil servants whose only expertise was to maintain law and order.

Soon after the nationalisation fiasco, there were waves of strikes in Karachi and other industrial towns of the country. Those strikes were crushed ruthlessly by the administrative machinery of the state after Bhutto announced that there was a war 'between the street power and the state power'. Bhutto did not allow full fundamental rights, and refused to lift the state of emergency which had been imposed by General Ayub Khan. He failed to repeal Ayub Khan's Press and Publications Ordnance, which allowed banning of newspapers and magazines and even confiscation of printing presses and property of the papers. He also did not dissolve the National Press Trust, which under the government supervision controlled many of the newspapers in Pakistan.

Bhutto could not provide *'roti, kapra aur makan'* to every poor family in Pakistan. But he did try to provide land to landless peasants. The seven *marla* scheme, giving seven *marlas* of land to every landless peasant, introduced during the Bhutto government was the most popular scheme among the poor. He could not provide employment to all the unemployed, but during his rule the route to the Gulf opened up, where hundreds of thousands of Pakistani workers are still earning much more than they could ever earn in Pakistan. Above all, Bhutto gave a sense of pride to the poorest of the poor in Pakistan. Bhutto's internal critics generally accused him of spoiling the poor, the man on the street. *"Yeh kammi ab aankh uthakey dekhtey hain"* (these menials now dare look us in the face) the rich used to complain.

Operation Fair Play may have been designed to help them. General Zia in his eleven years of rule never gave them cause to complain. His critics may be right when they say that Operation Fair Play took away the pride from the people. Those who tried to look the regime in the face had to face lashes and jail sentences.

Notes

In addition to sources acknowledged in other chapters, the following books have been found useful;

Shahid Javed Burki, Pakistan under Bhutto 1971-77, Macmillan, London, 1980
Lawrence Ziring, Pakistan: The Enigma of Political Development.

Boulder, Colorado, 1980, and also From Islamic Republic to Islamic State in Pakistan, in Asian Survey, XXIV, 9, (September 1984)

Hamza Alavi, p90-91, Political Economy of Praetorian State, in Pakistan: the Roots of Dictatorship, ed. H. Gardezi and J. Rashid, Zed Press, London, 1983.

Khalid B. Sayeed, Politics in Pakistan. The Nature and Direction of Change. Praeger, New York, 1980.

Lawrence Ziring (ed), The Subcontinent in World Politics, Praeger, New York, 1982.

Z.A. Bhutto, If I am Assassinated, New Delhi, 1978.

5
Zia - The Ringmaster

Martial Law did bring relief to the common people. Ordinary people, particularly those living in the cities, had got tired of street demonstrations, of police lathi-charges, of tear-gassing and firing. The businesses had come to a standstill. The daily wage earners, the rikshawallahs, the tongawallahs, the taxi drivers had all lost their earnings. Martial Law came to the rescue. Normal life which had been paralysed for quite a few months started gaining normality. The people were relieved and many were actually happy when General Zia announced in unambiguous terms that the general elections would be held in October of the same year, and the army would go back to barracks.

General Zia assured the people that he had taken over only to stop the warring factions from cutting each others' throats. He had come only to stop the bloodshed. He would hold free and fair elections as an impartial referee, hand over power to the elected representatives of the people and go back to barracks where, he said, he belonged. In his interviews to foreign correspondents he was fond of saying, "By Jingo, you will see elections held in October", and he invited several of them to come back in October, be his guest and see free and fair elections held in Pakistan.

In his address to the nation later in July, he assured the people that the constitution of 1973 had not been abrogated and the elections would be held under the same constitution. The 1973 constitution had only been suspended, he said. Earlier on July 15, General Zia had had long meetings with Mr. Bhutto and Maulana Mufti Mahmood, the leader of the opposition in the National Assembly before it was dissolved prior to the 1977 elections. They were both detained separately in Murree, and General Zia in his meetings with them is reported to have assured them as well that he had no political ambitions, had taken over reluctantly and his only job was to hold free and fair elections.

People generally believed him. He did not look a long-term ruler. Moreover General Zia had an immense capability of making others believe in his sincerity. Even shrewd politicians tended to believe him. The Soviet President Andrei

Gromyko is quoted as saying that at the time of Brezhnev's funeral, in November 1982, General Zia went to Moscow and the new General Secretary of the Soviet Communist Party, Mr Andropov, was angry because of Pakistans' involvement in the Afghan resistance against the Soviet-backed Kabul government and expressed his indignation to the General. The General took his hand and said with all sincerity, ''General Secretary, believe me, Pakistan wants nothing but very good relations with the Soviet Union''. Mr. Gromyko says they believed him, but sadly found out later that his words were not followed by actions. The Indian Prime Minister Rajiv Gandhi, like Mrs. Gandhi before him, has the same complaint that General Zia's assurances were never followed by actions. Yet if they tended to believe his words, it is no wonder that the politicians in Pakistan believed him. They had more reason to believe Zia's promises, since Bhutto along with other detained leaders of the People's Party and of the Pakistan National Alliance were quickly released from preventive custody. They started in earnest preparations for the forthcoming elections.

THE ELECTION CAMPAIGN

Political activities had been banned under Martial Law, but political parties had not been banned. They were finally banned in October 1978. The People's Party and the component parties of the Pakistan National Alliance, therefore, started making preparations for the October polls. Martial Law regulations prohibited open air political meetings, but indoor meetings were allowed. Bhutto, who had gone to his home-town of Larkana after being released from detention, came to Lahore on August 8, 1977, to address one such meeting. His public reception in Lahore was tremendous. Journalists present in Lahore at the time said that it was unprecedented in the history of the city. Bhutto addressed his party workers there and reportedly again played the American card. The United States was unhappy with him, he said, because he wanted Pakistan to have a nuclear reprocessing plant to meet its energy requirements. The then United States President, Jimmy Carter, claimed Bhutto, was angry with him because his government gave its whole hearted support to the cause of the Palestinians, for the establishment of a free and independent Palestine. The conspiracy against him, he alleged, was initiated by the United States administration.

Later in the same month, on August 28, Mr. Bhutto had a long meeting with the General and later said that the meeting had been arranged on his request, as he wanted to convince General Zia of the impending dangers to the unity of Pakistan. Bhutto maintained the very integrity of the country was in danger.

Bhutto had perhaps by then come to realise that he could face the generals only with the support of the people. This realisation came too late.

THE GENERAL'S TURNAROUND

No one can say with certainty now, as both the General and the late Prime Minister are no longer there to tell what transpired in their two-hour meeting on August 28, 1977, but soon after that meeting a chorus for "accountability" started. The first salvo was fired by retired-Air Marshal Asghar Khan of the Tehrik-i-Istiqlal, who had earlier been instrumental, or so it is claimed, in wrecking the proposed agreement between the People's Party and the Pakistan National Alliance. On August 30, Asghar Khan told a news conference that the people demanded Bhutto's trial and the verdict of the court first, before they chose their representatives. Accountability first, elections later, he demanded. Then the Jamaat-i-Islami came out with a statement with the same demand. The Muslim League and other political parties followed suit. The General, according to his own account, was an impartial referee. Bhutto was not in power, he could pose no danger. In a free and fair election the component parties of the Pakistan National Alliance could come to power and, acting within the constitution, could have arrested Bhutto and his associates and put them on trial. They did not do that.

They provided General Zia, though, with an opportunity to act, and on September 3, within days of the starting of the accountability movement, Bhutto was arrested. He was taken into custody at his Clifton residence in Karachi and taken to Lahore. He was charged with complicity in the murder of a political opponent, Mohammad Ahmad Khan Kasuri, who had earlier been murdered in Lahore. He was no opponent of Bhutto. Kasuri's son, Ahmad Raza Kasuri was a worker of Bhutto's People's Party and had got elected to the National Assembly on the bandwagon of the People's Party in the 1970 elections. He dissented with Bhutto and left the party. The police charge was that Bhutto wanted to get Ahmad Raza Kasuri assassinated and that the Federal Security Force, a creation of Bhutto, planned to murder him. The plan, it was said, went wrong as it was not he but his father travelling in the car which was waylaid by assassins, and instead of Raza Kasuri, his father became the victim of Bhutto's wrath. No journalist except those who were later hired by General Zia to write White papers on Bhutto's misrule could tend to believe it. Ahmad Raza Kasuri had never been a political figure of any stature what-so-ever. He still is not, despite the glare of publicity which that case allowed him. The poor man did not pose a threat to Bhutto. There were others who did. Khan Wali Khan, the veteran nationalist leader was one of them, who had been arrested and was being tried when General Zia staged his Operation Fair Play.

Bhutto was however arrested and produced before a court. His lawyers filed a bail application before the Lahore High Court and Mr Justice K.M. Samdani allowed the bail application saying that the evidence submitted by the prosecution was only circumstantial. Bhutto was released on bail. That was August 13, but four days later on August 17, he was rearrested − this time under a martial law regulation, (which could not be challenged in any court of law), and the General announced that Bhutto and his associates would be tried by a military court. He said that after going through the secret files he had come to know that Bhutto and his colleagues were guilty of murder and had failed the peoples' trust.

In the first week of October 1977, the General abruptly postponed the election for an indefinite period. In an address to the nation he said that the country was facing a grave danger, and could not afford the luxury of elections. And, according to him, the people wanted first the results of the "accountability". Earlier on August 15, in an earlier address to the nation, the General had said that the process of democratisation had begun, and had warned that any one who tried to hinder that would be severely dealt with. However, along with the postponement of the elections, further limitations were imposed on political activities.

Perhaps now some political leaders sensed that the General's game was different. But not all. Even an astute politician like Khan Wali Khan started singing the same tune. He along with his other colleagues, notably Ghous Bux Bizenjo, the former governor of the province of Baluchistan, and Arbab Sikander Khalil, the former governor of the North West Frontier, had been arrested by Bhutto and were being tried by a special tribunal in Hyderabad, Sind. In December 1977 General Zia released them and dissolved the special tribunal that had been trying them for sedition. After coming out of detention, Wali Khan's first public statement was − 'accountability first, elections later.'

Khan Wali Khan and his father, the late Khan Abdul Ghaffar Khan, the Frontier Gandhi, had never been able to gain popular support in Pakistan. They were never accepted by some key groups, the Punjabis and Muhajirs, (refugees from India who migrated to Pakistan after the partition, who always tended to look towards the centre for their survival). Nevertheless, because of their sacrifices and sufferings, their integrity was never questioned. Why then did Khan Wali Khan do that? He had always been a champion of democracy in Pakistan, and had undergone tremendous sufferings for it under successive regimes. Why did he not demand elections first, accountability later? He and his father earlier during Ayub Khan's Martial Law and then during Yahya Khan's Martial Law, were known to have been invited to collaborate. On both occasions they had refused. No one could accuse Khan Wali Khan of being hungry for power. Mr. Bhutto had made an enemy of him by dismissing the government of Baluchistan, a coalition government of Wali Khan's National Awami Party and Maulana Mufti Mahmood's Jamiat-ul-Ulema-i-Islam. As a result a coalition government of the same parties in the Frontier Province had resigned in protest. Mr. Bhutto had also talked much of rats and foxes. In one of his speeches in the National Assembly before his deposition, he had said that if Khan Wali Khan was a fox of the mountains, he was a rat of the desert. It was generally speculated at the time that the provincial government of Baluchistan had been dimissed under pressure from the Shah of Iran, who was concerned with the implications of a nationalist government in the Pakistani part of Baluchistan on the population of his Iranian Baluchistan.

Some believed Khan Wali Khan's action was a Pathan vendetta, that he was influenced by the so-called Pushtun 'gang of three', all members of Zia's kitchen cabinet. These were Ghulam Ishaque Khan, whom General Aiz had promoted from the post of secretary Ministry of Defence to the hurriedly created post of Secretary-in-Chief to the government of Pakistan, General Fazle Haq who was governor of the North West Frontier Province and later its Chief Minister, and Roedad Khan, the then secretary, Ministry of Interior.

Soon after general Zia's take-over, Mr. Bhutto's wife, Begum Nusrat Bhutto had filed a petition in the Supreme Court of Pakistan challenging the imposition of Martial Law. The Chief Justice of the Supreme Court was Mr Justice Yakub Ali whom the General had praised in his first address to the nation on July 5 1977. He had said that before taking the action, he first went to the Chief Justice and asked his legal opinion. But when Begum Nusrat Bhutto's petition came to the Supreme Court for hearing Mr. Justice Yakub Ali was removed, and replaced by Mr. Justice Anwar-ul-Haq who came from Jullundur, the same town in India from which General Zia came, and who was known to be his close friend. Judges of the High Courts were summoned within twenty-four hours to take a fresh oath of office. In November the Supreme Court delivered its judgement on Begum Bhutto's petition. The judgement upheld the imposition of Martial Law, declaring it legal and saying that it was necessitated by the prevailing law and order situation in the country prior to Martial Law. It, however, directed the martial law government to hold elections as soon as possible under the 1973 constitution.

Whether it was the politicians' furore for accountability before elections, or the unexpected public reception of Bhutto in Lahore, which prompted General

Zia to postpone the October 18 elections, is difficult to know. But many people now believe that the General had his plan ready when he took over the reins of government, and had been astutely following the plan when he announced the postponement of the elections in early October. The late Mr. Justice Safdar Shah was one of them. Chief Justice of Peshawar High Court, Mr. Shah had opted for early retirement as Mr Bhutto's government was believed to be unhappy with some of his decisions. Soon after Anwar-ul-Haq's taking over as the Chief Justice of the Supreme Court Mr. Justice Safdar Shah was offered a seat on the Supreme Court. A few years after resigning his position, Mr. Justice Shah gave an affidavit in a court of law whch, among other things, said:

"In hindsight it seems that right from the first day when the General imposed martial law in the country, he had ulterior motives and that he was simply buying time in order to defuse the frenzied mood of the people, who had taken to the streets in protest against the rigging of elections by the government of Mr. Zulfikar Ali Bhutto. For instance, he went back on his solemn pledge of holding elections by declaring that he would make the diverse elements of the society account for their misdeeds which so frequently brought about the collapse of democratic government and, second, that he would like to introduce Islamic laws in Pakistan. As to the process of accountability, he published what is called a white paper in which hundred of names of the alleged delinquents had been mentioned and to which document international publicity was given. After the lapse of about four years, however, he has taken account from only one person, namely Yahya Bakhtiar, the former Attorney General of Pakistan, who had courageously conducted the appeal of the executed Prime Minister in the Supreme Court."

Several leaders of the Pakistan National Alliance, who by demanding accountability first and elections later gave General Zia a pretext to postpone the October elections, now publicly admit that they fell in the trap. Professor Ghafoor Ahmad, a leader of the Jamaat-i-Islami and the opposition spokesman during the People's Party and the Pakistan National Alliance talks in mid-1977, has since said in several press statements that had the agreement reached between the two sides been signed and acted upon accordingly, democracy would have been restored in Pakistan.

THE BHUTTO TRIAL

Bhutto was charged of complicity to murder a political opponent and was tried by the Lahore High Court. It finally sentenced him to to death on March 19, 1978. The Chief Justice of the Lahore High Court was Mr. Justice Mushtaque

Hussain. He was a judge in the Lahore High Court during Bhutto's government, but had been superseded and not made the Chief Justice, as was his due in order of seniority. He happened to be in London when General Zia overthrew the civilian government and imposed martial law. He was reportedly contacted on behalf of the General, and told to return to Pakistan immediately as he had been appointed the Acting Chief Justice of the Lahore High Court as well as the chief election Commissioner.

Bhutto was tried in an open court but his defence plea was held in camera. The prosecution charges and the evidence of the prosecution witnesses were widely reported in the Pakistan press, but not a word of Mr. Bhutto's defence plea. During the trial the Chief Justice, Moulvi Mushtaque Hussain actually used to address press conferences telling the journalists of Bhutto's alleged crimes. Bhutto filed several petitions during the trial that the Chief Justice, by publicly expressing his views on the merits of the case, had debarred himself from judging him. All those petitions were rejected, and the verdict of guilty was given.

Later the same month, Bhutto filed an appeal in the Supreme Court challenging the judgment of the Lahore High Court. When the appeal came up for hearing, there were nine judges on the bench. One of them, Mr. Justice Qaisar Khan, reached the age of superannuation during the early stages of the hearing, and was not given any extension as was the norm – this was reportedly because he had given his view in open court on the fragility of the prosecution case. Another judge, Mr. Justice Wahiduddin Ahmad could not complete the hearing, as he suffered a stroke and was incapacitated. Among the seven judges left who heard the appeal one was Mr. Justice Safdar Shah whose affidavit to a court of law has been quoted earlier. In the same affidavit, he reveals that during the hearing of Bhutto's appeal a hotline had been installed in the chamber of the Chief Justice connecting him directly with General Zia, Mr. Justice Safdar Shah says:

> "During the hearing of appeal, a hotline telephone connection was installed in the chamber of the Chief Justice, connecting him with the General directly. This was wholly unprecedented because no judge of the Supreme Court, in view of the concept of independence of judiciary, is ever expected to have a line of communication with the Chief Executive, more so when the Chief Executive happened to be a martial law administrator."[1]

The Supreme Court rejected the appeal and upheld the judgement of the Lahore High Court by a majority of four to three. Mr. Justice Safdar Shah later said that the majority judgment had obvious factual flaws which were pointed out in the review petition filed by Bhutto. "For instance, the majority judgement had proceded, while reconstructing the scene of firing, on the assumption that one inch is equal to ten centimetres. It was enough to make the highest court of the country appear ridiculous'', wrote Mr. Safdar Shah. He also said that the Chief Justice, Mr. Justice Anwar-ul-Haq, acknowledging the reservations and doubts of the dissenting judges, suggested that in the judgment on the review petition a clear recommendation be made that the former Prime Minister should not be executed. The Supreme Court dismissed the review petition of Bhutto, but in the judgement did recommend that the General should not execute the former Prime Minister, but instead commute his death sentence.

Choudhry Fazal Ilahi, who was President of the country during Bhutto's time, had been allowed to continue in the office by General Zia, apparently to show that the constitution was being adhered to, and that there was continuity. Choudhry Fazal Ilahi was a civilian politician, and having had a long political association with Bhutto could have used his powers of clemency.But Ilahi's term ended in September 1978 and General Zia, who had stepped in only as an ''impartial referee'', took over as the President of the country. He was now the Chief of Army Staff, Chief Martial Law Administrator and he was also the President. The General often repeated his claim that he had taken over so as to establish rule of law in the country, and in Mr. Bhutto's case would abide by the judgement of the Supreme Court. Zia apologists have tried to exonerate him by saying that he merely upheld the verdict of the independent court. They conveniently forget that the judgment of the court was split, but the recommendation to commute the death sentence was unanimous.

Despite appeals of clemency from almost all the capitals of the world and the recommendation of his country's Supreme Court, General Zia confirmed the death sentence. Just after midnight on April 4 1979 Bhutto was hanged in Rawalpindi Central Jail, and his body secretly flown to his home town of Larkana to be buried. When the news broke out of Bhutto's hanging, his corpse had already been buried in his ancestral graveyard.

DEALING WITH THE OPPOSITION

To the western media, General Zia was something of a clown till he hanged Bhutto. The same year the Soviet Union invaded Afghanistan and General Zia became a darling of the west. He was soon seen as a benign, benevolent dictator. To President Reagan of the United States and other western leaders, the General became 'the last bastion of the free world'. He was portrayed as an affectionate family man, a loving father, a pious man. Even the senior Indian journalist, Khushwant Singh, is all praise for him. In a recent article he has written about

Mr. Ghulam Ishaq Khan and President Zia praying together. Ishaq Khan was the only civilian leader to support Zia's take-over in 1977 and stoody by throughout his rule.

his meetings with the General, saying that he always came to the door to receive him and came to the car to bid him farewell. He was indeed courteous, not only to journalists, but to all those who came to see him. Even diplomats were impressed with his courteous, humble manners.

His friends used to say that the General had to be harsh to be kind. But to innumerable mothers in Pakistan whose sons were publicly flogged, the General was not at all kind. On a number of occasions a microphone was actually placed near the mouth of the man being flogged, so that the assembled people could hear his cries and groans. And those who were flogged were not always criminals, murderers or rapists. They were often simple political workers incapable of dislodging General Zia by any other means, who expressed their frustration in graffiti. They just wrote slogans on the walls calling for the end of martial law and for democracy. Many hundreds of them were flogged, and thousands sent to jails where they were not treated as political prisoners. They did not receive the privileges allowed under Pakistan's Security Act. The political prisoners were at least allowed a bed, a reasonable financial allowance for their meals, plus a small monthly allowance for their daily necessities. For some ordinary criminals, the regular judicial process was open. They could be tried in open courts, and had the opportunity to prove their innocence. But those who wanted democracy had violated martial law, and had to be given an exemplary punishment so that others could be deterred. Martial law is hardly new to Pakistan. There was Ayub Khan's martial law. Then there was Yahya Khan's martial law. They were also dictators, not benign or benevolent. Political workers opposed to martial law and dictatorship went to jails and many of them were detained for many years — but they were not flogged and humiliated in the eyes of their brothers and sisters. Under Zia that seemed to become the norm.

Those who went to jail for violating martial law were often subjected to inhuman tortures. In a report entitled 'Torture in the Eighties', the London-based human rights organisation Amnesty International, said it had detailed reports which indicated frequent torture of prisoners in Pakistan. "Prisoners who have been subjected to torture include political party workers, trade unionists, teachers, students, journalists and lawyers'' said the report.[2]

A human rights organisation in Pakistan, the Political Prisoners Release and Relief Committee, signed affidavits of over one hundred and fifty political prisoners who had been tortured by the martial law authorities. In its report of 1986, the Committee stated; "the tortures range from solitary confinement to sustained beatings, water ducking, introducing chillies in the rectum, electric shocks, deprivation of sleep for long periods, burning the body with cigarettes, beating of the genitals and threats to relatives and so on. There appears to be no lower limit to the bestiality of the martial law authorities in their war against political dissent''.[3]

During Ayub Khan's martial law, one political activist had died while under interrogation in Lahore Fort, a detention centre used by the British during the Raj. He was Hasan Nasir, a leader of the banned Communist Party. There was such a furore over his death that the all-powerful Ayub government had to exhume his body to try to prove the prosecution point that he had committed suicide and was not killed. During Zia's martial law, many more died during police and army interrogation. They included the student leader Nazir Abbasi, the trade union worker Inayat Masih, and the political workers Mehr Chandio and Kalu Brahmin and Qamar Abbas. They are known to have died in interrogation centres, while scores of others died in the so-called "encounters" with the security forces. The Political Prisoners Release and Relief Committee has listed fifteen centres used by the security forces to torture political prisoners. They are; Chuna Mandi (Lahore), Shahi Qilla (Lahore), Kot Lakhpat Jail (Lahore), Muchh Jail (Baluchistan), Attock Army Fort (Punjab), Warsak Army Camp (Frontier), Bala Hisar Fort (Peshawar), Malir Cantonment (Karachi), Baldia Centre (Karachi), Karachi Central Jail, Field Investigation Unit Centre (Lahore), Lal Qi a (Lahore), Crime Branch Centre (Quetta), Khalili Camp (Quetta) and Field Investigation Unit Centre (Karachi). During the eight years of Zia's martial law there were said to be only a few lucky political prisoners who were not taken off to those centres.

Then there were what the lawyers called judicial murders. A Baluch student called Hamid Baluch was sentenced to death, but when the man he was supposed to have killed appeared in the court the Baluchistan, High Court ordered the military court which had passed the sentence not to implement its judgement. The Court order was not obeyed, and Hamid Baluch was hanged.

Another case was Ayaz Sammo, a trade union worker in Karachi who in 1984 was accused of the murder of a pro-Zia politician. The prosecution submitted the confession of the accused, which he told the summary military court had been obtained under duress. The prosecution also submitted blood samples of the assailant, who was wounded and bled as he fled from the scene. The blood samples of Ayaz Sammo were different from the blood samples of the murderer acquired from the scene of murder, and Ayaz Sammo had no trace of a wound upon his body. Ayaz Sammo was hanged in June 1985.

Then there was the case of Ayub Malik, Muhammad Essa and Saifullah Khalid. They were allegedly involved in the hijacking of a Pakistan Airlines plane in 1981. They were tried by a military court and sentenced to various prison terms. A retrial was ordered in August 1984, apparently on the orders of Zia. The military court retried them and sentenced them to death, and the General confirmed the death sentence on October 6th, 1984.

On the petition filed by Begum Nusrat Bhutto in 1977, the Supreme Court had upheld the validity of martial law on the basis of the doctrine of necessity. But it had declared the constitution of 1973 to be the supreme law of the land and had upheld the right of the civil courts to review the verdicts of the military courts headed by major and colonels. In October 1979, the General amended the constitution by a decree. The Constitution (Second Amendment) Order declared illegal the political parties, also making the military court superior in the constitution. This allowed the martial law authorities to transfer any case from civil to military courts and debarred civilian courts entirely from entertaining appeals from military tribunals.

Later, General Zia, embarking upon his Islamisation programme, introduced Shariat or Islamic courts. Thus the legal structure in Pakistan during the martial law period became three-tiered. The paramount law was martial law. At the second level there was Shariat or Islamic Law and on the third was the ordinary civil law. The relationship between the three was hierarchal in the sense that all cases could be tried by military courts, some cases and particularly Shariat cases could be tried by Shariat (or Islamic) courts, and only ordinary cases could be tried under civil law. The position of the accused was also different in these different courts. In a civilian court under civil law, the accused was considered innocent until proven guilty by the prosecution. However, in Shariat courts as well as in military courts, the accused was presumed guilty unless otherwise proved.

To further curtail the powers of civilian courts, the General introduced yet another amendment to the constitution in 1981. That was the Provisional Constitution Order which changed the constitution of 1973 almost altogether. Under that constitutional order the judges of the Supreme Court and High Courts were made to swear personal allegiance to the President and Chief Martial Law Administrator, who was General Zia himself. Several judges refused, while some were not called to take the fresh oath. Thus the civil judiciary also became nearly as subservient to the General as were the military courts. The repression, however, continued unabated. The lashings and the floggings remained the order of the day. In 1983, in the Karachi jail alone, more than two hundred political workers were allegedly flogged over a period of a few weeks.

CMLA — CANCEL MY LAST ANNOUNCEMENT

Soon after the hanging of Mr Bhutto, General Zia announced another date for the postponed general elections. They were scheduled to be held on 17 November, 1979. Announcements were again made that the elections would be held as scheduled. Warnings were again issued that no obstructions would be tolerated in the process of the revival of democracy. But in October of the same year, the promised elections were again postponed. That time the postponement was accompanied by still harsher measures. Till then the country had been living in what could be described as a twilight zone of martial law co-existing, albeit uneasily, with a measure of political freedom. The postponement of the elections in 1979 was accompanied by a total ban on political activities and on whatever press freedom was in existence. All the political parties were banned and the press was placed under censorship. A few component parties of the Pakistan National Alliance had until that point been co-operating with the General. Members of the Muslim League (Pagara Group), of the Jamaat-i-Islami, of the Jamiat-ul-Ulemai-Islam and of the Pakistan Democratic Party had joined the first civilian cabinet General Zia had formed in 1978. The second postponement of the elections and the banning of political parties alienated them also from the military junta. They dissociated themselves from the government. Although Zia retained tacit support of the Jamaat-i-Islami, which believed that the General was sincere in his Islamisation programme, and the Muslim League (Pagara Group), which had traditionally gravitated around power at all times, General Zia eventually lost their trust as well.

MOVEMENTS AGAINST MILITARY RULE

In the early stages of martial law, when all the other political parties were demanding accountability, the only party struggling against the military rule was Bhutto's People's Party. The PPP naturally bore the brunt of the repression. Hundreds of its workers were flogged and put behind bars. It was only after the second postponement of the elections that the other political parties finally came to realise that the General had ambitions other than those he had been publicly professing. Leaders of nine political parties then met in Karachi, and on February 6, 1981, they signed a declaration announcing a united front against the military rule. An umbrella organisation, the movement for the Restoration of Democracy (MRD) was launched. Most of the rival political figures joined hands to fight for the restoration of democracy.

The nine parties which came together were (1) the People's Party under the leadership of Bhutto's wife, Begum Nusrat Bhutto, (2) the Muslim League (Qasim Group at the time known as Khawaja Khairuddin Group), (3) the Jamiat-ul-Ulema-i-Islam of Maulana Mufti Mahmood, (4) the National Awami Party of Khan Wali Khan , (5) Pakistan Democratic Party of Nawabzada Nasrullah Khan, (6) the Pakistan National Party of Mir Ghous Bux Bizenjo who had earlier disassociated from Wali Khan's National Awami Party and had formed his own party, (7) the left-orientated Kisan Mazdoor Party of Fatehyab Ali Khan and (8) National Democratic Party of Sirdar Sherbaz Mazari and (9), the Qoumi Mahaz Azadi of Meraj Mohammad Khan who had formerly been a prominent leader of the People's Party and Bhutto's designated political heir. He had become disenchanted with Bhutto and formed his own political party which leaned towards the left.

Politicians in Pakistan have a tendency to join hands against military or authoritarian rule. The tradition was set by the politicians in the erstwhile East Pakistan, who had formed the first united front against the then authoritarian rule of the Muslim League. That was the Jagto Front which defeated the Muslim League in the 1954 provincial elections. Then during the movement against Ayub Khan they formed the Democratic Action Committee, and against Bhutto they formed the Pakistan National Alliance. In the Movement for the Restoration of Democracy (MRD), almost all the political forces of various shades joined hands. This comprised Muslim fundamentalists like the JUI, centrists like the Muslim League, nationalists like the National Awami Party and the Pakistan National Party and leftists like Qoumi Mahaz Azadi and Mazdoor Kisan Party. Only the Muslim League (Pagara Group), the extreme fundamentalists Jamaat-i-Islami, the Tehrik-i-Istiqlal of retired air marshal Asghar Khan and the Jamiat-ul-Ulema-i-Pakistan of Moulana Shah Ahmad Noorani remained outside its fold.

From 1980 Pakistan was seen from outside very much as a front-line state deserving strong support. But after the formation of the MRO, the General had for the first time become jittery. He felt power slipping from his hands. But he was provided with another God-sent opportunity. A passenger plane of the Pakistan Airlines was hijacked in 1981 and taken to Kabul, where one of the passengers was killed. A terrorist organisation, Al-Zulfikar, led by Bhutto's young sons, Murtaza Bhutto and Shahnawaz Bhutto, claimed responsibility. The People's Party became suspect in the eyes of other politicians and the opposition alliance, though not disbanded, became dormant. Begum Nusrat Bhutto and later her daughter Benazir left the country, ostensibly for medical treatment, it was seen as self-exile. The opposition movement to a great extent came to a standstill. However, it did not die. In 1983, while Benazir was still in the country but in detention, the Movement for Restoration of Democracy launched its first mass-campaign against the military rule, which was ruthlessly crushed. The campaign was mainly centred in the province of Sind, where the Punjabi army had no hesitation to shoot the Sindhi protesters dead. The campaign failed to spread to other parts of the country. There were few demonstrations in Lahore where, cunningly, force was not used. According to press reports at least one thousand people died in Sind in that movement. It had to be called off and it was.

Hundreds of political activists were jailed after the hijacking of the PIA plane in 1981, and then again in the opposition movement in August 1983, yet the opposition to military rule continued. It manifested itself in an extraordinary way in April 1986 when Benazir Bhutto returned from her self-imposed exile. It looked as if the whole of Punjab had turned out to receive her in Lahore. The opposition movement was revitalised, and it looked to some as if the Zia regime was tottering. But totter it didn't. Benazir proved to be a great crowd-puller, her public meetings attracting record numbers of people. They were, however, not prepared to face bullets. Her call to the people to come out on the streets in late 1986 proved to be a total flop — and it showed too how the PPP still lacked organisation. Moreover her attitude of confrontation angered other leaders of the component parties of the Movement for the Restoration of Democracy. After this failure, Benazir seems to have decided to go along with the other parties of the alliance.

During Zia's time the control of the authorities was helped by the Islamisation programme. Islam in the sub-continent has many different sects, with their respective religious practices creating rivalries. The strongest challenge came from the Twelver (or Imami) Shias. In 1980, tens of thousands of Shias converged on the city of Islamabad to protest against what they called an imposition of the Sunni brand of Islam. General Zia conceded their point and made Shias exempt from the changes, but nevertheless carried on with his Islamisation programme which was by that time opposed even by the Jamaat-i-Islami, his onetime closest ally. And before Zia's death even the Pagara Muslim League had gone against him.

However, the sectarian and regional feelings aroused by the policies of the Zia government effectively served to divide the opposition. For the first time in Pakistan, Shias organised their own political party, the Tehrik-i-Nifaz-i-Fikah-i-Jafferiah. The Muhajirs, for their part, organised themselves for the first time in an organisation of their own, the Mohajir Qoumi Movement. It has since developed into such a formidable force that in the latest local elections it gained overwhelming majorities in the two biggest cities in Sind, Karachi and Hyderabad. Pathans and Punjabis in Sind formed their own organisations too, so as to counter the Mohajir organisation.

Sind seems to be increasingly fragmented into rival ethnic groups, with the situation particularly serious in Karachi, a metropolis of some ten million people coming from all the ethnic groups of the country. Since 1984, Karachi has been the scene of recurring communal riots between Pushtuns and Mohajirs. There has been a collapse of law and order in some crowded slum areas of Karachi, caused by ethnic tensions and the activities of Pushtun drugs traders. The easy availability of automatic weapons, as a by-product of the Afghan war, has helped fuel violence.

Disaffection in Baluchistan in the 1970s was rightly considered to be the major source of danger for Pakistan's fragile unity. From 1983, it has steadily become apparent that Sind has taken over from Baluchistan as Pakistan's problem province. Developments in the interior of Sind have taken a very different form from those in Karachi, Hyderabad and other urban centres of Sind.

The extremely violent uprisings in many rural areas of Sind which so disturbed

49

the regime in 1983 were led by activists of the small radical party Sindhi Awami Tehrik, which gained ground in this important southern province long dominated by the PPP. The party's leader is Rasul Bux Palejo, a Maoist-style agitator who suffered long imprisonment. The party's radical political ideas, "an eclectic blend of Sindhi nationalism and marxism", appealed not only to oppressed peasants, but also to students and other people also of the towns of Sind. Sindhi politics is fragmented, but realignments are changing its shape. The Sindhi Awami Tehrik merged with the left-orientated Awami National Party (ANP), led by Khan Wali Khan and with a strong Pushtun following in NEWP. Rasul Bux Palejo became general secretary of ANP. The veteran Sindhi nationalist G.M. Syed is leader of the Sind National Alliance, a grouping of smaller parties. There is growing support in youth circles for the nationalist demand of 'Sind for the Sindhis', the separatist goal of a Sindhi homeland originally expressed in the Sindhu Desh movement which developed in the 1970s.

Sindhi nationalism is based essentially on resentment at the power and wealth of non-Sindhis settled in this province since 1947. The Sindhi sense of grievance has steadily grown, especially among the youth. A series of bloody clashes took place in 1988, with Sindhi gangs attacking the Urdu-speaking mohajirs, so-called "New Sindhis", as distinct from the "Old Sindhis". According to some mohajirs, these riots in towns of Sind could have been provoked by the authorities. The Sindi-mohajir relationship had remained uneasy every since earlier riots between the two groups in the early 1970s, when the PPP moved to change the status of the Urdu language. However, most realised the two groups had to co-exist.

The assorted grievances of the ethnic minorities against successive Punjabi-dominated regimes provided a rallying-point for Sindhi-Pushtun and Baluch nationalists. The sheer weight of the Punjab − with some 65 per cent of Pakistan's total population, and much of its wealth too − partly explains Punjabi predominance. The Punjabis' preponderance in the armed forces, though, is the key element in their power.

The formation in August 1985 of the Sindhi-Baluch-Pushtun Front was intended to help towards a radically-reorganised Pakistan. It was designed as a clear break with the past political set-up − so unsatisfactory as far as minority leaders were concerned. This Front took in most active nationalist and separatist groups with local backing in the three minority provinces of Sind, NWFP and Baluchistan. In its projected Constitution for the country, the Front insisted on a confederal system reserving very wide powers to the four constituent provinces of Pakistan, as the sole way of satisfying minority grievances.

The Sind-Baluch-Pushtun Front pledged that the minorities would stay with

Pakistan, instead of aiming at independence, provided full provincial autonomy was conceded. In this visionary Constitution, each of the four provinces would have equal representation in an elected legislature and a newly-raised and - recruited army. The armed forces would remain under central control, but with its present command structure broken up. This vision is likely to remain a Utopia.

These sectarian and regional tendencies did provide a setback to the opposition movement but despite the division between various Muslim sects and the divisions between the Sindhis and the Punjabis, between Mohajirs and Pathans, Baluchis and Punjabis the people of Pakistan seem to have no love for authoritarian rule. That is why, perhaps, the Movement for the Restoration of Democracy is the most formidable force in Pakistan today, with the parties outside trying to come into its fold. Benazir was reportedly negotiating with Mohajir Qoumi Movement leaders and those of Jamaat Islami in mid-1988.

ZIA'S SEARCH FOR LEGITIMACY

General Zia had absolute power. He retained almost total support of the armed forces, which he called his constituency, and initially, at least, he had also the support of the political parties opposed to Bhutto. His rule, however, did not acquire legitimacy. He called elections in 1977, perhaps in the hope that the People's Party was discredited, the Pakistan National Alliance was a loose umbrella organisation of divergent political parties. If the PNA won, its leaders could be manoeuvred into accepting him as head of state. The PNA-dominated national assembly could elect him as the president. But Bhutto's reception in Lahore showed General Zia very clearly that the PNA parties were not going to win.

He again called elections in 1979 but they were perhaps a decoy to defuse the situation after the hanging of Bhutto. He kept on playing with politicians, though. In 1978 just after one year of martial law, he formed a civilian cabinet with leaders of some of the component parties of the PNA. Soon after Bhutto's hanging there started a game of what has been described by journalists as ''prime ministerial musical chairs''. General Zia is known to have offered the prime ministership of the country to Ghulam Mustafa Jatoi, to Khan Wali Khan, to Pir of Pagara and according to some reports, to retired air marshal Asghar Khan as well. Jatoi and Khan Wali Khan are known to have refused. It is not certain whether the other two refused or were just not called in.

The search started again in earnest after the MRD movement of 1983. The government was surprised by the suddenness and intensity of the agitation and felt genuine fear of its spreading to Punjab. Some pro-establishment journalists at the time saw an American hand in the movement and a remark of the then United States Defence Secretary was often quoted in which he said that in the current difficult situation the United States might have to look for an alternative. The Americans may not have been interested in the MRD movement, and may well not have been looking for alternatives. But General Zia did have to look for alternatives. In 1984, he announced a referendum and general elections on a party-less basis. Despite having been crushed during the 1983 movement, the MRD was a formidable force and could alter the course of the elections had it decided to take part.

The MRD leaders today agree that the boycott of the elections did not prove to be a good strategy. There was an MRD summit to discuss strategy. The Tehrik-i-Istiqlal of retired air marshal Asghar Khan had also joined the MRD by then. At the MRD summit in Abbotabad, a majority of the MRD leaders were for participation in the elections. Jatoi who at the time by virtue of the absence of Begum Nusrat Bhutto and her daughter, Benazir, represented the People's Party — he later split and formed the National People's Party — Khawaja Khairuddin of the Muslim League, Ghous Bux Bizenjo of the Pakistan National Party and Maulana Fazlur Rahman of the JUI were in favour of participation. But the so-called 'three Khans' — Nazrullah Khan of the Pakistan Democratic Party, Wali Khan of National Awami Party and Asghar Khan of the Tehrik - opposed it and carried the rest with them. The MRD perhaps at the time failed to realise that by calling elections, General Zia was in a position of no win. Party-based or party-less polls, they were most likely to be won by the component parties of the MRD. General Zia had only one option. He could have postponed the elections yet another time and would have been a butt of ridicule.

The opposition boycott of the referendum was mostly effective, but that of the elections to the national assembly and provincial assemblies in February 1985 failed. Many of their own activists ignored the boycott, and offered themselves as candidates. People did vote in the elections, and the elected assemblies came into being. And after being elected a majority of non-party Assembly members became party members again. They joined the Pagara League whose nominee was the Sindhi landowner Mohammad Khan Junejo, whom General Zia chose to be his Prime Minister.

The elected government and martial law co-existed for nearly nine months. Journalists were often told during that time that Junejo was his own man, that he was not playing second fiddle to the General, that he had removed the seemingly powerful General Mujeeb from the Ministry of Information, and that he was taking the country back to democracy — cautiously but surely. The fact of the matter is that Junejo and his band of politicians were junior partners in the power game. That was vividly shown when Junejo and his colleagues in the National Assembly not only gave blanket approval to all the measures that the General had taken since taking over, (including the deposition of an elected Prime Minister, which, under the constitution of 1973, was an act of treason,) but also passed an amendment to the Constitution granting General Zia absolute powers to dismiss the elected government and dissolve the elected assembles.

Junejo and his colleagues gave him the rope which the General effectively used to hang them on May 29, 1988. Mr. Junejo has always claimed credit for the lifting of martial law on December 31, 1985. The claim, however, does not seem to have any substance. Why would General Zia need martial law when the elected assembly had given complete approval with retrospective effect to all his measures, and given him additional powers to disband the assembly itself?

But when Junejo and his elected band of politicians were playing General Zia's game and could not pose a threat to him, why did he dismiss the elected government and dissolve the assemblies? There are some intriguing theories; one of them is that the Vice Chief of Army Staff, Gen. Aslam Baig was a Junejo appointee, and that with his connivance Junejo was going to depose General Zia. A second theory is that Junejo was about to release a cabinet committee report on the Ojhri arms depot blast earlier in 1988 which put the blame squarely on senior army officers close to Zia. The arms depot at Ojhri camp, Rawalpindi (which was reportedly used as a transit centre for U.S. arms going to Afghan guerrillas), exploded on 10 April, 1988 killing more than one hundred people and destroying a huge quantity of ammunition, besides millions of rupees worth of property. The cause of the blast is not yet known, nor has the Junejo cabinet committee report yet seen the light of the day.

There was another incident in Rawalpindi soon after the Ojhri camp blast. A young army officer was beaten by a group of civilians who alleged that the officer had passed indecent remarks at their womenfolk. The officer is reported to have come back with a group of fellow officers and beat the civilians, who included a member of the Punjab provincial assembly as well. The civilians were then arrested and Junejo apparently intervened to obtain their release on bail. This sequence of events is said to have angered the military high command.

Then there were the Geneva accords, on Afghanistan, which Junejo supporters say were signed by Pakistan in spite of Zia's opposition to them. Before the signing of the accords, Junejo had called a special conference of the opposition political leaders, at which General Zia was bitterly criticised by almost all the opposition leaders present.

These are all conjectures. What is certain is that Pakistan was going through a crisis. Law and order had virtually broken down in parts of the province of Sind. There were almost daily bomb explosions in the province of Frontier. Junejo government's latest annual budget had angered the merchants and the middle class urban population alike. Though some of its harsh measures were withdrawn, the public was angry. There was the Ojhri camp explosion and an armed confrontation between a group of army officers and civilians which showed that the patience of the civilians was running thin.

General Zia-ul-Haq needed a scapegoat. He knew the Junejo government had no popular base. It had given him absolute power but not the legitimacy he so badly desired. Perhaps the new assembly would have given him that. Hence the announcement of another election although Zia had all along vehemently rejected the opposition call for an early election. And under him this time also the elections would have been on a non-party basis. However, the assembly would, in all likelihood, have been more-broad-based than before, since the opposition parties were keen to contest these elections, in whatever form they were held. As President and Chief of Army Staff, Zia already held power, but a broad-based elected assembly could at last have given him a measure of legitimacy − something the General had wished for throughout his career in politics.

Notes

1. Affidavit dated 28 May 1981, published in Report by Political Prisoners Release and Relief Committee of Pakistan, Lahore, 1986.
   also see Victoria Schofield, Bhutto: Trial and Execution, London, 1979.
2. Torture in the Eighties, Amnesty International, London, 1982.
3. Report by Political Prisoners Release and Relief Committee of Pakistan, Lahore 1986.
4. Pakistan. Human Rights Violations and the Decline of the Rule of Law. Amnesty International, London, 1982.

6
Continuing Rivalry: India and Pakistan

One of President Zia's last decisions, taken just before his death, was to confer on Morarji Desai, the former Indian Prime Minister, Pakistan's highest civilian award NISHAN-I-PAKISTAN. The citation praised Mr Desai for his "commitment and services to the promotion of ties between the two countries". The award − announced on Pakistan's forty first birthday (14 August 1988) provoked a heated debate in India as it was seen by many, particularly in the ruling Congress (I) party, as yet another gimmick by the shrewd General to embarrass Prime Minister Rajiv Gandhi. Although Mr Desai accepted the award and thanked President Zia for honouring him, supporters of Prime Minister Gandhi felt the real aim of the Pakistani gesture was to indirectly blame Rajiv Gandhi for the poor state of relations between the two neighbours.

There is little doubt that one important factor behind General Zia's decision was to impress the people of Pakistan and India by his goodwill gesture. It was certainly a skilful diplomatic move to outflank Rajiv Gandhi in public relations. Mr Gandhi earlier bestowed on Pakistan's rebel Pushtun leader Khan Abdul Ghaffar Khan India's highest honour 'Bharat Ratna'. Nevertheless it is true that India's relations with Pakistan were better under the short-lived rule of the Janata Party government led by Morarji Desai. One may disagree with Mr Desai who claims credit for the normalization process that was evident during this rule. But it is also true that his attitude to the Zia-regime was significantly moderate. How could Zia forget that Mr Desai was one of the few world leaders who failed to criticise the hanging in Pakistan of the former Prime Minister Zulfikar Ali Bhutto in 1979.

In fact the normalization process seen during the Zia-Morarji period was a follow-up of what Prime Minister Bhutto and the Indian Prime Minister Mrs Gandhi had started with the signing of the Simla Accord in 1971. After the humiliating defeat of Pakistan by India in the second full fledged war in 1971 (the first being in 1965) which resulted in the break-up of Pakistan and creation of Bangladesh, Bhutto desperately felt rapprochement with India should be one of the first priorities of his government. Abandoning his vow to fight India for one thousand years, Bhutto came to see Mrs Gandhi at the Indian hill resort Simla, along with his young daughter Benazir. The agreement he signed there with Mrs Gandhi provided for the withdrawal of Pakistani and Indian forces from the occupied territories. Even more important was the fact that both countries agreed to solve the Kashmir problem bilaterally; this had been the major issue between them ever since partition.

Although India-Pakistan relations were not without tension in the following years, the process which started with the Simla Accord resulted in an exchange of ambassadors before Bhutto was deposed by General Zia in a coup, and Mrs Gandhi was defeated by Mr Desai's Janata Party in the general elections of 1977. In this respect Benazir Bhutto is right when she claims that her country had better relations with India during her father's democratic regime.

In February 1978 the then Indian Foreign Minister Atal Bihari Vajpayee visited Islamabad. During his visit an important accord on the Salal Dam was finalized which sought to safeguard interests of both countries regarding the flow of river Chenab waters. The accord itself was signed in New Delhi after two months. It is worth noting that negotiations for this agreement were started some eight years before, but were finalised at a time when the Bhutto trial was taking place and General Zia desperately needed public support at home.

NEW CONFIDENCE

The real turning point in Pakistan's foreign relations came when the Soviet Union invaded Afghanistan. It re-established Pakistan's role as a 'bulwark against communism' and rehabilitated General Zia both at home and abroad. It was followed soon after by Mrs Gandhi's return to power in India. These two events revived the historical mistrust and rivalry between India and Pakistan as the Afghanistan factor tremendously increased the confidence of General Zia. The process of normalization of relations that began under the Bhutto regime, received its first major setback. The election victory in the United States for President Ronald Reagan was an added boost for him. Although Mrs Gandhi did not condemn the Soviets for their invasion of Afghanistan, she was clearly alarmed by this extraordinary development. She was shrewd enough to realise the dangers of a superpowers' war by proxy on India's doorstep. But at the same time she did not adequately use her influence on the Soviet Union for the withdrawal of its forces from Afghanistan. Actually India failed to play any effective role in the solution of the Afghan problem, despite its good relations with both Kabul and Moscow. It was only when the Geneva agreement was in sight that Rajiv

Gandhi suddenly seemed desperate to play a role. Indeed, Mr Gandhi had ruled out any Indian initiative for resolving the Afghan conflict in his well-publicised press conference in New Delhi in January 1987. One can sympathize with India's concern about the uncertain nature of a future government in Kabul, but Rajiv Gandhi's diplomatic manoeuvring just before the Geneva Accord appeared politically immature and lacked cohesion.

General Zia's successful negotiations with the Reagan administration for a massive 3.2 billion dollar military and economic aid package over six years began a new phase in adverse relations between India and Pakistan. Mrs Gandhi saw this military aid as a threat to India's own security. Indian concern on this account was due to past experience. The U.S. military aid Pakistan received between 1954 to 1965 was used by Pakistan's military ruler General Ayub Khan for fighting a full scale war with India over the Kashmir issue. However, the Americans stopped military aid to Pakistan after this war for many years. From the Indian point of view this did not make a great deal of difference, since Pakistan managed to get military aid from China during this period and at the 1971 war. Events of 1971 also changed the U.S. policy as the Nixon administration found it necessary to support Pakistan in the wake of increased co-operation between India and the Soviet Union, especially after the Indo-Soviet treaty of August 1971.

This does not mean, however, that the West lost all hopes with India and started promoting once again Pakistan for looking after its interests in the region. Indeed, the 1971 war proved that India was the dominant power in South Asia. In 1978 the U.S. Presidential Security adviser used the term 'new influential power' to describe India.[1] This reassessment was the result of a number of factors: India's nuclear explosion of 1974 and the growing insecurity of Western interests in the region following events in Iran, Afghanistan and Pakistan.[2] At the same time the hanging of Bhutto increased General Zia's isolation in the world, leading to a substantial cut in aid for Pakistan. It is not at all surprising that around the same time (September 1979) Pakistan joined the Non-aligned Movement.

LIVING WITH ELDER BROTHER

The Soviet invasion of Afghanistan also did not change the Western perception of India, though it substantially increased the importance of Pakistan and General Zia. This is explained by continued improvement of India's relations with the West. Although a major improvement came after Mrs Gandhi's son Rajiv became Prime Minister, following his mother's assassination in 1984, Mrs Gandhi's stance was also not as harsh against the West as it had been during her earlier regime.

Even China recognised India's role as the main power in South Asia, though it remained suspicious of Soviet ties with India. Mr Deng Xio-ping himself was quoted in the Indian press as saying in early 1981 that he regarded India as the 'elder brother' of South Asia.[3] A similar trend in thinking was also seen among some at least of Pakistani leaders at that time. An important figure in Bhutto government, Ghulam Mustapha Khar, who was living in Britain in exile at that time, argued in an article in THE ECONOMIST (31st Oct. 1981) for a long-term Pakistani deal with India. It was not clear whether he was speaking for himself or for some policy-makers in the United States, as Tariq Ali prefered to interpret Khar's comments in his book 'Can Pakistan Survive'. Ali wrote:

> The point is, however, they (Khar's comments) did not fall from the sky. They represent the thinking of an important layer of policy makers in the United States, and also inside the Pakistani civil service. Khar presented his option as way of preventing total dependence on the United States, but this involved some sleight of hand, since there can be little doubt that the long-term interests of the USA dictate one strong state in South Asia rather than two. India is potentially a far more powerful defender of capitalist interests in the region than either the Shah's Iran was or a military-dominated Pakistan could ever be.[4]

Nevertheless Mrs Gandhi's scepticism about the real intentions of Pakistan and the United States did not simply fade away. As a result, when General Zia proposed to Mrs Gandhi a non-aggression pact to counter her attacks in 1981 on Zia's negotiations for a 3.2 billion dollar military and economic aid package with the United States, she responded in a very cool manner. Mrs Gandhi saw this proposal as a smoke screen designed to extract more and more military aid from the West. All these sophisticated weapons, she argued, that Pakistan was obtaining in the name of defending itself from Soviet aggression could eventually be used against India. Alternatively, she later proposed a treaty of peace, friendship and co-operation to Pakistan similar to the Indo-Soviet treaty of 1971. General Zia did not reject her proposal outright, though his response was equally cool. Indeed Pakistan saw the Indian proposal as nothing more than a counter-propaganda initiative.

President Zia's meeting with Mrs Gandhi in New Delhi in 1982 did help in creating a better climate. The two agreed to create an Indo-Pakistan joint commission. Subsequent meetings between the officials of the two countries did speak about progress and improvement in relations, but there was nothing concrete to boast about. Actually bilateral relations started deteriorating from

1984. Two factors contributed to this: the Sikh terrorist problem in the Indian state of Punjab and Pakistan's Nuclear programme. The Nuclear factor was not a new source of tension between the two neighbours, but the upsurge of the Sikh factor was a new phenomenon.

SIKH FACTOR

There has been a long history of India and Pakistan attacking each other for interference in one another's internal affairs. Inflammatory reports about Pakistani nationals arrested "while trying to incite communal riots" have been quite common in the Indian press since Pakistan was created in 1947. Similar reports have also been appearing in the Pakistani press. Most of the time, however, attacks on each other by Indian and Pakistani leaders are aimed really for domestic consumption. One important factor behind the recent attacks on Pakistan by Indian leaders, accusing it of aiding and abetting the Sikh extremists in the Punjab, was certainly to hide their own failures in solving the problem. On the other hand, Pakistani leaders have also been busy accusing India of creating trouble in its Sind province.

India does indeed have sympathy with the Sindhi nationalists. Mrs Gandhi herself inaugurated the World Sindhi Sammelan (Conference) in 1983 in New Delhi, where some speeches were seen as a provocation in Pakistan. President Zia only one month before his death had claimed that Pakistan had proof that India had tried to foster violence between ethnic Sindhis and Mohajirs (Muslims who went to Pakistan after partition.[5] This allegation was taken by many, though, as a counter-propaganda offensive, since Zia did not say what the proof was.

The Indian accusations of Pakistan helping the Sikh extremists increased in number and volume soon after the Indian army action on Amritsar's holiest Sikh shrine the Golden Temple in June 1984, to flush out the terrorists. After a bloody battle, which enraged the Sikh community worldwide, the army did succeed in its mission. The large number of weapons which the army seized in the action, claimed India, bore signs that they were smuggled in from the bordering areas of Pakistan. The Zia government always denied Indian allegations, but this did not stop India making even more frequent attacks on Pakistan in this regard. The Hijack of two Indian airplanes by the Sikh extremists to Lahore later that year further worsened bi-lateral relations.

After the assassination of Prime Minister Indira Gandhi in October 1984, General Zia tried to charm her son and successor Rajiv Gandhi in particular and the Indian people in general.

He came to Mrs Gandhi's funeral in New Delhi and announced three days' official mourning in Pakistan — incidentally, a gesture Gandhi returned when Zia died. Indian policy, however, towards Pakistan has not changed during Rajiv Gandhi's regime. Indeed the tensions between India and Pakistan have increased since Rajiv Gandhi came to power after winning the December 1984 elections. India's Sikh problem still remains the major factor. His own government in New Delhi, and also the Punjab state government in Chandigarh, have frequently claimed to have 'concrete proof' of Pakistan's hand in the Punjab problem. But this 'proof' has only recently been given to the Indian parliament and the press in the form of some captured documents.

These documents, claim the government, were seized during the ten day police action at the Golden Temple in Amritsar in May 1988. According to Indian Home Affairs Minister Santosh Mohan Dev, these documents revealed that leaders operating from Pakistan had been sending instructions and large supplies of sophisticated weapons to terrorists in Punjab. The government also claimed that one of these documents contained a clear indication of a plot to assassinate the Prime Minister Rajiv Gandhi and the Home Minister Buta Singh. Pakistan, of course, denied all knowledge of this alleged plot or the existence of these documents. As further evidence of Pakistani help to Sikh extremists, Indians have frequently reported the capture of Sikhs illegally entering into India across the border from Pakistan.

Although the Indian population by and large believe in Indian claims about Pakistani help to Sikh terrorists, it is very difficult for an independent observer to check the validity of Indian evidence. Reasons for long delays in producing evidence also remain unexplained. On the other hand some Western journalists believe there are at least some grounds behind the Indian allegations. There appears to be at least an official blind-eye towards the Sikh terrorists crossing the border into Indian Punjab.

India has also alleged that there are training camps for Sikh terrorists in Pakistan. This charge has also been repeatedly denied by Pakistan, but the well known Pakistani writer Tariq Ali has given weight to the Indian charge, saying that it is no secret, these camps are situated in the vicinity of Peshawar and have even apparently become an unofficial tourist attraction.[6] It is also a well known fact that easy availability of arms in Pakistan's illegal markets since the Afghan conflict began has attracted all sorts of buyers including the Sikh extremists from Indian Punjab. The Pakistan government at least had not ruled out the smuggling of arms and drugs across the border in to India. In the eyes of the Indian public, Pakistani complicity with regard to Sikh extremism remains the major single issue between the two countries at present. And no matter who remains in power in India and Pakistan, this single issue is likely to dominate their relations in the near future.

NUCLEAR AMBITIONS

The second most important issue is Pakistan's nuclear programme. Unlike the case of Pakistan, the Indian nuclear programme is much advanced and nearly four decades old. It was started soon after independence under the leadership of India's first Prime Minister Jawahar Lal Nehru, who use to take a keen personal interest in the scientific development of the country. In 1974 India exploded a nuclear device and with this success entered into the club of the few elite nations who had this technology. This incident shocked Pakistan, whose foreign policy had always been affected by events in India. Although Pakistan set up an Atomic Energy Committee in 1953, it was not until this committee was upgraded to become Pakistan Atomic Energy Commission, with Dr Ishra Husain Usmani appointed to its board by the Military government of General Ayub Khan in 1958, that the programme was really started. However, it was Zulfikar Ali Bhutto who gave Pakistan's nuclear programme a goal. Alarmed by the Indian advancements in this field, he declared in his much quoted speech in Pakistan's National Assembly: "If India builds the bomb, we will eat grass and leaves, even go hungry. But we will get one of our own, we have no alternative."

Pakistan's military defeat by India in 1971 came as a shock to the country but for Bhutto it brought power. This defeat also made Bhutto more resolute than ever to fulfil his nuclear dream, as it confirmed his fears about India. One month after being appointed as Pakistan's President in January 1972, Bhutto reportedly told the country's top scientists, at Multan in the Punjab, that Pakistan must develop its own nuclear bomb.[7] Before he was deposed by General Zia in 1977, Bhutto set the pace of Pakistan's nuclear programme running at full speed. The nuclear programme may have little significance for Pakistan's illiterate masses, but it was highly favoured by the country's armed forces who lost all their prestige, morale and even power after the 1971 defeat.

It was precisely for this reason that General Zia continued with the nuclear programme started under the Bhutto regime. He even encouraged the country's nuclear scientists to speed up their work as the Afghan bonanza brought undreamed of financial resources for the country's military. As a shrewd operator, Zia also realized that his services for the anti-Soviet cause would soften criticism in the West in the wake of media revelations of Pakistan's nuclear programme.

To a large extent General Zia proved right. The aid that the Carter administration cut for Pakistan as a punishment for its nuclear ambitions, came back with compound interest following on the Soviet invasion of Afghanistan. Although the nuclear issue did force the Americans to attach severe conditions on aid to Pakistan, it did not prevent Pakistan going ahead with its programme. Even those conditions placed on aid were imposed mainly after intense lobbying by India.

The concern in India about Pakistan's nuclear programme is explained by the fact that Rajiv Gandhi, during his first visit to the USA in June 1985 after becoming Prime Minister, repeatedly attacked Pakistan for its alleged Nuclear weapons programme. After that he hardly missed any opportunity to repeat this charge. For its part, General Zia's government always denied the charge, claiming its nuclear programme was for peaceful purposes. However, in 1987 Pakistan's top nuclear scientist Dr Abdul Qader Khan admitted for the first time to an Indian journalist, Kuldip Nayar, that Pakistan did possess a nuclear bomb. The sensational interview was published in London's OBSERVER newspaper on March 1, 1987. The newspaper quoted Dr Khan as saying:

"What the CIA has been saying about our possessing the bomb is correct and so is the speculation of some foreign newspapers . . . they now know we have done it."

Although Dr Abdul Qader Khan later denied this interview, it was widely believed to be true. It created a furore in India. Later Rajiv Gandhi announced that his country would also consider its nuclear options in view of Pakistan possessing the Bomb. On several occasions, there have been heard rumours in both countries that India − with or without the help of Israel − might attack Pakistan's nuclear installations, in spite of an agreement to the contrary signed in New Delhi in December 1985 between President Zia and Prime Minister Gandhi.

CRICKET DIPLOMACY

Credit may go to General Zia personally that in spite of a marked coolness in India-Pakistan relations during his time, and in spite of continued tension on the borders, the two neighbours did not go for another full-scale war. During the last two years, however, there have been fears that renewed skirmishes in the disputed Siachin glacier in remotest Kashmir might develop into a full war. The countries came again closer to a full-scale war when tension increased substantially between December 1986 and February 1987. It started with Indian Army large-scale exercises, code named 'Operation Brasstacks', in November

1986, in the desert of Rajasthan, just 37 miles (60km) from the Pakistan border. At the same time Pakistani forces were also engaged in their own exercises in the bordering province of Sind. Then in January 1987, both countries found their troops close to the Punjab border, directly facing each other. India claimed it was Islamabad which suddenly moved its troops in large numbers just at a time when Indian army exercises were in full swing in Rajasthan.

No matter who moved first, the situation suddenly turned very dangerous, creating speculation in the world media for possible consequences. 'The Times' in London even discussed what it called the 'seductive effect' of the Falklands factor. Its Delhi correspondent, in a story entitled "War could help both Gandhi and Zia", explained the factors which might push both leaders into the war, though in the same article this correspondent had to admit ". . . it seems unlikely that either side really thinks it could benefit from war. . ."[8]

Although good sense prevailed in both governments, and the war was avoided, it was General Zia who took the initiative to defuse tension. The Indian Prime Minister had been avoiding meeting him for a long time. In the prevailing circumstances, Gandhi was neither himself accepting Zia's long standing invitation to visit Pakistan, nor would he take the step of inviting Zia to New Delhi for official talks. The general, always a step ahead of the young pilot-turned-politician in public relations, once again outmanoeuvred him. Zia came to India — ostensibly to watch a cricket match between India and Pakistan. Zia's 'cricket diplomacy' reminded many journalists in India of the exceptional hospitality he had extended to them and other Indians on their visits to Islamabad. For the general Indian public, Zia's gesture was reminiscent of his earlier rhetoric on peace and friendship with the people of India. It is debatable whether either side wanted a military confrontation. Yet, there can be no doubt that it served as another timely reminder of the sensitive state of India-Pakistan relations. Many people in India and Pakistan would agree with Pakistani senator Javed Jabber who said in a speech to the Pakistani senate, just one week before Zia's death: "India-Pakistan situation is a unique example in the world whereby the people of both the countries desperately aspire for friendship and harmony while powerful vested interests both inside and outside the two governments hold them back."[9]

It was an impressive speech. However, the problem is not as simple as that. The fact is, 41 years of partition have been unable to bridge the gulf of mistrust between the two people. Despite numerous accords and meetings between the two governments during this long period, the mistrust has not vanished.

Hindu-Muslim riots in India always (and naturally) become headlines in Pakistan and attract unwelcome statements from Pakistani leaders. Indeed, it suits any military or non-military government in Pakistan to play the anti-India card. At the same time Indian leaders also never miss an opportunity to play the anti-Pakistan card, and unfortunately it must be said it suits them too. The Zia years were no exception to this tradition. His regime was always quick to express concern over the plight of any Muslims attacked in communal riots in India. It regularly outraged the Indian authorities, who saw it as an interference in India's domestic matters. On the other hand, statements by Indian leaders in sympathy with Pakistan's opposition movement MRD angered the Zia government.

The Zia period was, however, relatively calm over the Kashmir issue, which has traditionally been the most volatile dispute between India and Pakistan. Apart from some minor clashes between the two armies, the Kashmir issue did not add much to the tension.

India, of course, objected to Pakistani leaders' raising the issue at international meetings, in contravention of the Simla accord of 1972. India has also been very concerned about anti-India (or pro-Pakistani) agitations in the Kashmir valley, close to the northern border with Pakistan. It is worth noting that when General Zia first staged his coup and deposed Bhutto in 1977, there were anti-Zia demonstrations in Indian Kashmir, though later when he had established himself in Pakistan, slogans in his praise became a regular feature of anti-India demonstrations in Kashmir.

On Zia's death in August 1988, Muslim demonstrations in Kashmir turned very violent, with at least three people dying in police firing. It must be said, though that these demonstrations in Kashmir valley have more to do with the domestic politics in the Indian state of Jammu and Kashmir. The anti-India and pro-Pakistani slogans raised by Kashmiris are traditional forms of expressing dissatisfaction against their own state government. It is also not very surprising when we consider that these demonstrations are organised by fundamentalist muslim groups in Kashmir, whose policies have more in common with Pakistan's (largely pro-government) Jamaat-i-Islami than the secular parties of Indian Kashmir.

GANGING UP ON THE BIG BROTHER

Pakistan's policy with other neighbours in the subcontinent and the outside world has been also largely conditioned by its relations with India. Rivalry with India has always made Pakistan closer to countries having bad relations with India. In June 1987, when the Indian air force dropped a quantity of food, medicine and other relief supplies over Sri Lanka's Jaffna peninsula, so as to help the

Tamil civilians caught in fighting between the Tamil terrorists and Government forces, Pakistan led criticism by all the Indian neighbours for what it described as an infringement of international law and violation of airspace of Sri Lanka by India.

Sri Lanka, clearly angered by the unwelcome Indian action, circulated reports in the media that it was considering a request to Islamabad for help in setting up a new defence system to deter any future Indian air incursion. Within two weeks of this incident, Sri Lanka's National Security Minister, Lalith Athulathmudali made an unscheduled 24-hour stop-over in Pakistan, before his visit to Europe and the United States.

Before the India-Sri Lanka accord of July 1987 on the Tamil problem, India had been helping the Tamil rebels, and General Zia's government was actively supporting the Sri Lankan army with training and supply of military equipment. The Indian government has accused Pakistan during the Sri Lankan conflict several times of escalating tension there. Pakistan has also tried to forge good relations with Sri Lanka's Muslim minority, but while doing so it always tried to avoid antagonising the Sri Lankan government. For this reason Pakistan has also avoided criticising Sri Lanka for taking the help of Israel in training its forces in anti-guerrilla warfare, though the Israeli presence in Sri Lanka was bitterly criticised by the Pakistani press and the fundamentalist parties. The Pakistan-Sri Lanka relationship was strengthened by President Jayewardene's week-long visit to Pakistan in March 1985. General Zia also paid a visit to Colombo later the same year, in December 1985.

Relations with Bangladesh (part of Pakistan until 1971) have also considerably strengthened during the Zia regime. It actually took four years for the Bhutto regime to finally come to terms with the fact of independence and to recognise Bangladesh in 1974. But it did not delay recognising the new government in Dhaka following on the assassination of its first Prime Minister, Sheikh Mujibur Rehman. Indeed Pakistan was the first country to recognise the new regime in Bangladesh, helping it to become an ally of the Muslim world. However, it was after General Ershad came to power in a military coup in 1982, that a closer Pakistan-Bangladesh relationship developed. Significantly, General Ershad seems to have followed General Zia in the political tactics he adopted to deal with the opposition at home. Both his referendum and the process of Islamization in Bangladesh were very similar to what General Zia had already adopted in Pakistan.

Both the generals also played an active role in forming the South Asian Association for Regional Co-operation (SAARC), which was formally launched in Dhaka in December 1985. India only reluctantly joined the new organisation, since it was sceptical of the organisation's real purpose. Indians were of the impression that this regional grouping would be used by the smaller neighbours, led by Pakistan, to launch criticism of India.

India joined the Association only after making quite clear that no bilateral issues would be raised at SAARC. However, India has not been able to avoid indirect attacks by other SAARC member nations.

COMPETITION IN AFRICA

The traditional rivalry between Pakistan and India has extended far outside the subcontinent in the past decade, to take in African countries. India has maintained for a long time close relations with African and other countries of the Non-Aligned Movement, training military personnel and in some cases providing arms to governments. India has also supported guerrillas of some freedom fighting groups.

Under Zia's rule, Pakistan no longer quietly accepted this aspect of India's foreign policy. Pakistan has actively and successfully competed with India to provide military help in Africa, especially in southern and eastern Africa.

One interesting example has been Zimbabwe, where India and Pakistan competed with each other to provide economic and military help (albeit limited) to the guerrillas of ZAPU and ZANU, pitted against the white colonists' regime. Here General Zia scored one of his first diplomatic triumphs over India, by shrewdly deciding to support Robert Mugabe's ZANU party. In the 1980 elections which preceded independence, to many people's surprise Robert Mugabe won outright, going on to become Prime Minister. Pakistan won the thanks and trust of a grateful new government, going on to provide instructors for Zimbabwe's air force.

Mrs Gandhi had backed the wrong horse. Earlier India had provided military and economic help to both ZANU and ZAPU, but before the 1980 elections, she decided to back the rival ZAPU party of Joshua Nkomo instead.

Although this incident did not, in fact, significantly reduce India's importance in the eyes of the new government in Harare, it was, however, seen as a setback to Mrs Gandhi's effort in blocking Pakistan gaining a diplomatic initiative in a field India had come to regard as its own domain. It was perhaps the first hint to India that the general next door was also a skilful diplomat, and that the era of "tear-shedding" Pakistani diplomacy (as carried on under Bhutto) was finally over.

CONTINUING RIVALRY: INDIA AND PAKISTAN

Notes:
1. Braun, Dieter, "Changes in South Asian Intra-regional and external relationships", The World Today, October 1978.
2. Butt, Sri Kant, "India and the Third World: Altruism or Hegemony" Zed Books Ltd., London.
3. The Times of India, New Delhi April 9, 1981.
4. The Independent, London August 18, 1988.
5. The Guardian, London August 19, 1988.
6. Bhatia, Shyam, "Nuclear Rivals in the Middle East" RKP 1988, London.
7. The Times, London January 26, 1987.
8. The Times of India, New Delhi August 11, 1988.

7
The Afghan Muddle

The problem of Afghanistan dominated Pakistan's foreign relations from 1980. Pakistan gradually became more entangled in the affairs of its neighbour, as an Afghan civil war developed into a popular guerrilla struggle against a regime imposed by foreign forces. Firstly, a sketch of Afghan developments is necessary. An Afghan civil war followed the Saur revolution of 27 April 1978. This was a military coup in Kabul, led by military cadres of a small Afghan communist party (People's Democratic Party, or PDPA). In place of President Mohammad Daoud, a new regime was declared under a little known Pashto writer and veteran left-wing activist Nur Mohammad Taraki, as chairman of the Revolutionary Council and Prime Minister.

In July 1978 the small PDPA split, with the Khalq (Masses) faction coming out on top. A purge followed of their rivals of the minority Parcham (Banner) faction, with the joint-deputy-Prime Minister Babrak Karmal, together with six other leading Parchami figures sent abroad as ambassadors. Other Parchamis, in common with thousands of independent-minded members of the Afghan intelligentsia and army officer corps, were imprisoned or exccuted by the Khalq regime.

The PDPA regime's indiscriminate brutality under Taraki and his aide (and later in 1979 his successor as President) Hafizullah Amin alienated many in the Afghan capital who had early on welcomed a change from the dictatorship of Daoud. The Khalqis did develop, though, support among the educated youth of both sexes, at Kabul University, the Polytechnic and the high schools concentrated in the capital and major towns.

In March 1979, a mutiny of the army garrison and a general uprising in the important western city of Herat was quelled only by massive-scale repression, including air raids on the city. From the spring of 1979, armed opposition was roused by a misguided attempt to spread the revolution into the countryside, where the PDPA had virtually no support. A series of drastic changes by decree were brutally implemented by zealous Khalq cadres in many rural areas, together

A young Afghan refugee woman, one of millions, living in Pakistan, raising her family and waiting to return home.

Photo: Courtesy of UN-HCR

with beatings or murders of local rural notables. They succeeded only in further alienating farmers and landless peasants alike, suspicious of changes coming from the capital.

Pakistan's relations with the new regime in Kabul deteriorated badly from the spring of 1979. The mounting internal problems faced by the regime were blamed on interference by Pakistan and Iran, with unsubstantiated claims that large units of soldiers from these countries had "invaded" Afghan territory. A shrill propaganda war by radio between the PDPA regime and its neighbours was the nearest they came to actual hostilities.

What is undeniable is that within months of the Saur Revolution, Pakistan's frontier cities of Peshawar and Quetta had become the HQs in exile of the resistance. This was a wholly predictable and natural development.[1]

Some of the opposition figures emerging as leaders had already arrived in Pakistan in the mid-1970s, after Prince Daoud had taken power from Zahir Shah and declared himself President. Indeed, some of this small group of Afghans had been backed by the Bhutto government, armed for an unsuccessful adventure in 1975 to provoke uprisings in various regions inside Afghanistan. This was in response to Daoud's help for dissident Baluch tribesmen of Pakistan, but also part of the inherited rivalry between the two states, expressed in Kabul's promotion of "Pushtunistan".

For this core of exile Afghan Fundamentalists, and many more Afghan nationalists with political ambitions arriving after the April 1978 coup, Peshawar represented an ideal centre from which to organise. It was very close to the Pushtun borderlands, with access to many of Afghanistan's most populous provinces. The Pushtun (Pathan) tribal population of North West Frontier Province (NWFP) − like Baluchistan to the west − still has much in common with their fellow Pashto-speakers across the Durand Line, a British created frontier arbitrarily cutting across tribes.

The exile parties' actual power to affect events across the border was in practise only slight in the period before 1980. Their activists were few in numbers. The rural uprisings challenging the PDPA regime which took place in many areas inside Afghanistan in 1979 and 1980 were led by individual commanders and internal fronts, often quite independent of the parties based in exile.[2]

All the Afghan exile parties at this time lacked large resources with which to extend their influence and buy support inside Afghanistan. Small amounts of money, apparently from Saudi Arabia, were inadequate to buy more than tiny quantities of rifles. By far the most important source of arms for the exile parties, as for the independent internal guerrilla fronts, were at this time captured

71

convoys, army posts and the major arsenal of Herat, together with weapons from army deserters.[3]

Paradoxically, it was the Soviet Union which produced the impetus for rapid growth of influence on the part of the anti-communist parties.

More than anything else, it was, of course, the Soviet military intervention in Afghanistan in the last days of 1979 which stirred international interest in this strategically situated country on the borders of Central Asia, the Middle East and South Asia.

IMPACT OF SOVIET INTERVENTION

There were clear regional implications from the Soviet military intervention in Afghanistan, and the prospect of an indefinite guerrilla war. For all the regional states the Soviet military presence in Afghanistan was unwelcome. The scale of the fighting and destruction inside Afghanistan steadily widened from 1980, through mass resistance by the Afghan people and foreign intervention in the war. For the key neighbour states of Pakistan and Iran in particular, a massive influx of refugees caused serious economic, ecological and political problems, with some 3 million and 1.5 million refugees respectively by 1987.

Superpower rivalries added to the inherent instability of this volatile region. With some 115,000 Soviet troops based in Afghanistan, and new or expanded air bases under Soviet control 300 miles closer to the Gulf and Indian Ocean, it seemed to alter the regional balance of power. One of the war's indirect results was a build-up of sophisticated weaponry for Pakistan's armed forces during the 1980s, paid for by the USA and Saudi Arabia.

While Soviet actions in Afghanistan since 1979 were crucial, the policies of many foreign states jointly contributed to the conflict. Both the Superpowers, China and other states of the region tried with varying degrees of success to influence events.

Following the Soviet military intervention, a coalition of interests led by the USA, together with Saudi Arabia, Kuwait and China, provided arms and funding for the guerrilla resistance. The initial shipments of small quantities of infantry weapons were steadily expanded over the next years. US military aid reportedly grew sixfold to reach $250 million by 1985, and $470 million in 1986.

In this "arms pipeline", Pakistan, of course, played a crucial role. Distribution to guerrillas was the responsibility of the parties to whom were delivered the small arms. The seven major exile parties recognised by the Pakistani authorities eventually formed, under pressure from their foreign clients, an Islamic Alliance of Afghan Mujahidin.

THE AFGHAN MUDDLE

Geopolitical logic and Pakistan's own national interests arguably dictated the policy pursued by the military government from 1980. Pakistan's former Foreign Minister Agha Shahi, has cogently argued this case, at least, as have numerous other writers.[4]

The Afghan issue polarised opinions in Pakistan. Though many from the political opposition voiced strong criticism of the government's policy as mistaken and dangerous, it was difficult to gauge with any degree of certainty how far these views had solid support among the general public. In the early years of the Afghan struggle, at least, there was strong sympathy, and even admiration expressed among ordinary Pakistanis for the Afghan *jihad*. This early support undoubtedly waned, though, as the negative aspects of Pakistan's involvement became more obvious.

What is certain is that Pakistan's military ruler General Zia ul-Haq gained immensely in international prestige and by solid Western financial underpinning from 1980, as a direct result of Pakistan's role as a conduit for military help to guerrillas across the border inside Afghanistan.

From mid-1980, Western diplomatic and economic support began to be given unstintingly once again for Pakistan. US relations with Pakistan, which had reached their lowest ebb in 1979, slowly picked up. After four rounds of discussions, the USA offered in 1981 an aid package worth $3.2 billion for 1982-87. The same General whose trial and hanging of the fallen Prime Minister Bhutto, harsh martial laws and indefinite postponement of elections in Pakistan and the continuing nuclear programme had alienated friendly governments and the western media alike was soon seen as an essential ally — and by most as a benevolent, if stern dictator.

The Afghan opposition parties' freedom to organise in Pakistan, and to recruit at will guerrilla fighters from the refugee camps, was inevitably contrasted by Pakistani politicians with the rigorous banning of politics altogether under martial law. Many questioned the value and significance to the West of Afghan "freedoms", when these were being denied in Pakistan.

CONTEST OF SUPER POWERS

The goal, if not the means, of Soviet strategy in Afghanistan has been consistent. The USSR wanted political stability and a friendly government in place in Kabul. Moscow invested its military prestige as well as large funds for development and building of infrastructure in this backward land along the sensitive Soviet border with Central Asia.

The USSR had already established a dominant position in Afghanistan's economy a full decade before the 1978 coup in Kabul, with the mineral-rich region north of the Hindu Kush in particular becoming virtually a Soviet sphere of influence. Since 1979, closer links with the USSR's Central Asian states have served effectively to integrate Afghanistan into the Soviet economic system.

There has been speculation on the merits of 'Finlandization', a form of limited independence from the USSR, akin to that enjoyed by Finland. Spokesman for the Afghan resistance have consistently rejected the very notion of such an infringement of Afghanistan's independence. Many people of goodwill, on the other hand, argue that this would be a happy outcome of a brutal, pointless war.

It was questioned by others, though, whether Finland was not a special case, and whether the true parallel for Soviet long-term policy could be found in the case of Outer Mongolia; a weak, undeveloped and almost empty land which was, in all but name, a colony of the USSR. In some respects, Soviet strategy in Afghanistan recalls the neo-colonial policies followed in the Muslim lands of Central Asia.

US policy of support for the guerrillas enjoyed rare bi-partisan support in Congress. The small scale flow of weapons slowly but steadily increased from 1980. Afghan guerrillas in the early years of the struggle received only basic infantry weapons, in quantities which were relatively small by comparison with other major guerrilla wars of the Third World; "In January 1981, when the Reagan administration took office, the total annual cost of the covert operation of support to the Mujahidin was said to be $100 million, involving the United States, Pakistan, Egypt, Saudi Arabia and China. Interestingly, Saudi funding at that time exceeded that of the United States. Later on, an understanding was reached whereby Saudi Arabia was "matching dollar for dollar" American assistance."[5] In 1987 the U.S. Congress approved $600 million worth of aid, making it the largest covert operation mounted by the CIA.

The long debated decision, taken finally in 1986, to provide missiles for Afghan guerrillas to defend themselves against air attacks also marked a new and possibly decisive stage in the long war. The provision of Stinger and Blowpipe (respectively US and British-made) anti-aircraft missiles, together with training in their use in Pakistan, had an undeniable impact on the war, eroding the total air superiority of Soviet-Afghan forces. In spite of the small numbers of missiles provided to Afghan guerrilla groups, the military impact is estimated by most observers to have played a big part in the Soviet decision to carry out a phased withdrawal of troop from Afghanistan from May 1988, as agreed at Geneva in March 1988.

US policy over Afghanistan as it developed had its domestic critics. Hawks and doves competed for influence in Washington. The stridently anti-communist

THE AFGHAN MUDDLE

PROVINCE-WISE BREAK UP OF AFGHAN REFUGEES

(Population 000 Nos)

Province/Area	Population as on 31.3.1988			% age share
	Registered	Unregistered	Total	
NWFP/FATA	2196.9	200.0	2396.9	68.9
Baluchistan	655.2	163.3	818.5	23.5
Punjab (Isa Khel)	180.8	0.4	181.2	5.2
Sind (Karachi)	20.0	56.7	76.7	2.2
Azad Jammu & Kashmir	..	2.7	2.7	0.1
Islamabad	..	2.2	2.2	0.1
Not Accounted for	..	..	..	..
TOTAL	3053.0	425.3	3478.2	100.0

.. Not available.   Source: Minister of Frontier Regions & Kashmir Affairs and Pakistan.

lobby so influential under President Reagan favoured stepped-up support for what they judged a straightforward fight against Soviet expansionism, in which the USA could also score merit as being on the side of a mass-backed, Islamic cause.

A more moderate position within the US Congress and the administration favoured more caution about giving aid to a divided Afghan resistance, and wished more care to be taken not to alienate Pakistani public opinion. Strains in US-Pakistan relations grew again in 1987, over the old issue of Pakistan's nuclear energy ambitions, and a threatened suspension of the huge US military and civil aid programme.

Critics of US policy denied that the USA, and the West in general, were at all concerned with the heavy human costs which the warfare entailed for the Afghan people. They maintained that the USA was determined to fight on – 'to the last Afghan', regardless of the hopelessness of the struggle.

Defenders of the policy countered, though, that the Afghan resistance had, after all, started without any substantial foreign aid, and enjoyed a remarkable level of popular support. Opposition parties claimed to control over 80 per cent of the country, and denounced the government of the PDP as a puppet regime. In these circumstances, it was argued that the struggle would continue anyway, with or without foreign backing.

Many observers believed that the sole way to achieve a final settlement allowing the Afghan people a choice of government was to maintain military pressure on the USSR by aiding the Afghan guerrilla resistance.

PRESSURES ON PAKISTAN

Pakistan was from the very beginning an essential partner in the co-ordination of foreign support for the Afghan resistance. Foreign aid in the form of infantry weapons was channeled to the guerrillas via the Pakistani military authorities, which in turn distributed weapons to the seven recognised exile parties, as well as some independent guerilla fronts inside Afghanistan.

The destruction inside Afghanistan by air raids and bombardment produced a flood of refugees from 1980. Some of the economic costs of Pakistan's burden of being host to almost three million Afghan refugees were paid by relief aid from UNHCR and many foreign states, but other pressures steadily mounted. A series of terrorist bomb attacks, carried out by agents of the Kabul regime, killed or wounded many Pakistanis. Bomb incidents were frequent especially in NWFP from 1984, with blame often placed on the Afghan factor.

Scores of incursions over Pakistani airspace, as well as attacks on villages by Afghan or Soviet warplanes took place each year. This indirect military pressure undoubtedly brought home to Pakistanis the dangers of becoming a 'front-line state', and antagonising a super power. The miserable Afghan refugees inevitably became scapegoats for all the various problems associated with the Afghan war − not least the rapid expansion of the heroin trade, which actually benefits many extremely rich and influential Pakistanis, Pushtun and non-Pushtun, besides some Afghans. (The production by Pakistani "drug barons" of heroin from opium began only from 1980, in the Pushtun tribal borderland between Pakistan and Afghanistan.)

Pakistan's political opposition exploited the increasingly controversial issue of government support for Afghan guerrillas. Pro-Soviet parties organised demonstrations against Afghan refugees. The domestic repercussions of the Afghan crisis have been considerable in Pakistan, and there are many signs of a growing polarisation of opinion against what is often regarded as a US-dictated Afghan policy. Some Pakistanis feared the emergence of a second Lebanon in their country, with the Afghans as uprooted, well-armed Palestinians.

From the Pakistani opposition side, notably by the left-wing Pushtun leader

THE AFGHAN MUDDLE

Abdul Wali Khan of NDP, it was often demanded that the government should come to accept the Soviet-imposed PDPA government in Kabul, close the supply chain for the guerrillas and expel the exile parties, possibly together with the refugees. However, such a policy of appeasement of the PDPA regime would not only have gone against the geostrategic goal of ending, ot at least reducing, Soviet domination of Afghanistan, it would also have alienated Pakistan's closest allies and largest aid-givers − the USA, Saudi Arabia, China and the Western countries in general.

China has been an important supplier of infantry weapons to the guerrillas since 1980. The view from Peking is that the Soviet strategy is designed to drive a wedge between China and Afghanistan along their common border of just 50 miles, in the remote Wakhan − Little Pamir mountain region. The garrisoning of Soviet troops in the Wakhan from 1980 was seen as a potential threat to the Karakoram Highway, the land link between China and Pakistan. China has repeatedly denounced 'Soviet hegemonism' in Afghanistan as well as in Kampuchea, calling for the restoration of both countries' independence.

China was an important giver of economic aid to Afghanistan before the 1979 invasion but cut its aid to Kabul after that and showed consistent support for the resistance. Observers point, though, to China's slowly improving relations with the USSR, and recent reductions in Soviet troop levels in Outer Mongolia − a third source of friction between the communist giants. In the medium term, these could serve to reduce Chinese backing for the Afghan cause.

Annual resolutions in the UN General Assembly passed by overwhelming majorities condemned Soviet actions in Afghanistan, but in themselves they meant no more than did the ritual Palestine resolution. Critics of UN impotence to end this brutal war often failed to understand the limitations within which the UN has to work. It has no power to enforce resolutions, or decisions, unless and until key member states agree to underwrite its rare peacekeeping operations. Without some consensus of views, and a new willingness to compromise by all the states involved, and above all by rival Afghan leaders, no political agreement is really possible.

Afghan Resistance leaders complained bittlerly that their voice was simply being ignored at Geneva, and that for any peace settlement agreed there to stick, they too must consent to its terms. Their claims to be an integral part of the UN peace process, rather than be nominally consulted from time to time by itinerant UN envoys, received full support only from Iran, which refused on this specific ground to join in the UN-sponsored series of indirect talks between the three neighbour states.

THE MUSLIM WORLD

Iran has acted quite independently over the Afghan issue since 1978. As a neighbouring power with a long, open border and close traditional links, Iran pursued a policy without reference to Pakistan and the other pro-Western states backing the Afghan resistance. Iran's aid was limited and highly selective, with some small Shi'a groups active in central Afghanistan almost the exclusive beneficiaries of weapons and training. Iran's deliberate policy of creating its own Afghan forms of fervently Shi'a groups (known as Pasdaran, Hizbollah and Jihad Islami) proved counter-productive, by exacerbating tensions and rivalries within the imami Shi'a population of Afghanistan.

Iran proved stronger on rhetoric than action in supporting what was frequently praised in the Iranian media as a fully justified jihad (holy war) against an alien communist regime imposed by the USSR.

The major Sunni Muslim Afghan parties, (as well as the independent Shi'a party Harakat Islami, active in many areas of Afghanistan) were permitted to organise in the border city of Mashad, (itself a major centre of Afghan refugees), as well as other cities of Iran. However, they were severely hampered in crossborder operations into the Herat region. They faced restrictions on movement, and an adamant refusal by the Iranian authorities to allow more than a trickle of weapons to go in transit across the borders.

Tehran's preoccupation from the end of 1980 was bound to be its own war with Iraq, together with coping with a chaotic economy and building up an Islamic society. With an abundance of Great and Little Satans to combat – ranging from the USA, USSR, Britain and France to the Arab states backing Iraq – the Islamic Republic had good reason to think of the Afghan war as a sideshow.

There is no monolithic or co-ordinated policy towards the DRA, or Kabul government, by Muslim states. What most have in common, though, is broad disapproval of the Kabul regime which emerged in the wake of the Soviet invasion of Afghanistan in 1979. The leading conservative Arab states have been the most active, notably Saudi Arabia, Kuwait and also Egypt under Sadat.

Saudi Arabia supports the Afghan mujahidin as part of its Pan-Islamic policy, but also (like the other regional states) with the goal of blocking communist successes in the region. Much of Saudi financial aid – reliably said to amount to hundreds of millions of dollars each year – has gone to two fundamentalist-orientated Afghan parties, Hizb-i-Islami of Gulbuddin Hekmatyar and the so-called Unity led by Professor Sayaf.

Saudi Arabi was very active since 1979 in Islamic circles to get support for the Afghan jihad. Riyadh fully backed Pakistan's stand over Afghanistan. The conservative Arab influence was duly reflected in voting at sessions of the Organisation of the Islamic Conference (OIC). In January 1980, the OIC held its first extraordinary Conference of Foreign Ministers, in Pakistan's capital Islamabad, on the Afghan issue. General Zia gave the first of a series of public appearances in Islamic circles as a defender of the Afghan people's independence against Soviet aggression. The OIC member states called almost unanimously for the immediate and unconditional withdrawal of Soviet troops from Afghanistan.

The DRA representatives were not permitted to take up Afghanistan's seat in the OIC. Significantly, though, this seat has been held vacant ever since the Soviet intervention, from 1980 on. The OIC failed to turn it over to representatives of the Afghan Resistance, in spite of repeated impassioned requests by leaders of Afghan parties in exile, attending IOC sessions with the status of observers.

Even the normally pro-Soviet, Arab radical leader Colonel Muammar Qadafi of Libya publicly criticised the Soviet intervention in 1980. Predictably, the only uncritical friends of the USSR among all the Arab states over the Afghan question have been Syria and South Yemen. As for Algeria and Iraq, they took no public stand over the issue. For many Arab states, as for Muslim states in general, support for Afghan independence actually remained largely symbolic − less potent a symbol by far than the cause of Palestine, and remoter than the immediate problem and danger from the Iran-Iraq war.

Even more than in the West, the fighting inside Afghanistan has been only spasmodically reported in the Arab media. There is little detailed knowledge of the Afghan struggle, and little evidence of strong public interest or concern. It is mainly within Muslim fundamentalist circles that the Afghan jihad is given strong emphasis. The Afghan war has always remained overshadowed by the prolonged crisis in revolutionary Iran, first with the seizure of American hostages in Tehran, then by the Iran-Iraq war.

Such formal commitment as does exist within the Muslim world to the cause of an independent, non-communist Afghanistan stems in large part from the influence of Saudi Arabia and Kuwait. Together, these two oil-rich states fund the OIC, providing also much of its development funds for poorer Muslim countries. The governments of most Muslim countries are well aware how impotent they themselves are to affect events in distant Afghanistan.

Notes: The Afghanistan Issue

1. for further reading consult:
   Anthony Arnold, Afghanistan's Two-Party Communism: Parcham and Khalq. Stanford, California, USA: Hoover Institution Press, 1983.
   Raja Anwar, The Tragedy of Afghanistan, London, Verso, 1988.
   Henry S. Bradsher, Afghanistan and the Soviet Union, Durham, USA: Duke University Press, 1985.
   Bhabani Sen Gupta, Afghanistan. Politics, Economics and Society. London, Frances Pinter, 1986.
   Anthony Hyman, Afghanistan under Soviet Domination, 1964-84. London, Macmillan 1984.
   Olivier Roy, Islam and Resistance in Afghanistan. Cambridge, CUP 1986.
2. see Anthony Hyman, The Afghan Politics of Exile, in Third World Quarterly, vol 9, no. 1 (January 1987).
3. see Nazif Shahrani and Robert L. Canfield (eds), Revolutions and Rebellions in Afghanistan. Berkeley, USA, California University Press, 1983.
4. In Hafeez Malik (ed), Soviet-American Relations with Pakistan, Iran and Afghanistan. London, Macmillan, 1987.
5. Mushahid Hussain in Middle East International, London, 30 April 1988 and see 'The Arms Trade', in South Magazine, London, May 1987.

8
Shadow of the Crescent

Pakistan's relations with Muslim states certainly became stronger during the Zia years. Although Zia followed the broad policy of Bhutto in developing links with the Muslim world, there were some important differences.

After the 1971 break-up of Pakistan, there was a deliberate and new emphasis on the Muslim world to the west, at the expense of the subcontinent. But even here, Pakistan's rivalry with India continued to play a role. Ever since 1947, India has maintained close relations with the Arab world. One important objective in its foreign policy has been not to let Pakistan stand out as the sole spokesman of the subcontinent's Muslims.

Significantly, India never established diplomatic relations with Israel. India has been a firm supporter of the Palestine Liberation Organisation (PLO), along with other freedom fighting fronts in the Third World. Mrs Gandhi formed a close relationship with the PLO leader Yassir Arafat. In 1980 the PLO was granted permission to set up a diplomatic mission in New Delhi.

General Zia's own service in Jordan, as brigadier on secondment to the Jordanian army, was during a crisis in relations between the Jordanian ruler and the PLO. Zia was there at the time of "Black September", when King Hussein's forces drove the PLO out of Amman in 1970. It did not make for cordial relations with the PLO after 1977. Pakistani links with the PLO were correct, rather than close. Significantly, Yassir Arafat never visited Pakistan during the Zia years. His absence even from Zia's funeral in August 1988 must have been noted in the Muslim world. On the other hand Arafat was a frequent visitor to New Delhi during all those years. He was also one of the many foreign leaders who came to attend Mrs Gandhi's funeral in New Delhi in 1984.

PAKISTAN'S LINKS WITH THE GULF STATES

The relationship between Pakistan and the Gulf states developed remarkably in the economic and military fields during the Zia years. Pakistanis working abroad in well-paid jobs helped to prop up a weak economy, by sending home regular remittances, in particular to families in the Punjab and NWFP, where the bulk of the workers originated. The rupee value of US$ remittances rose sharply too from 1982, after the Pakistani rupee was delinked to the US dollar.

At the height of the oil boom, well over two million Pakistanis went to work in the Gulf region, the largest single group of foreign migrant labour in the Gulf, bigger than either Yemenis or Egyptions. Their remittances home provided one of the country's principal sources of foreign exhange, worth between $2.3 and $2.9 billion each year until the mid-1980s, equal to some 8 per cent of the GNP. It may be even higher. If money smuggled back into Pakistan is included, the true figure, according to some Pakistani sources, may have been closer to $4 billion annually at its peak in the early 1980s.

Even at the lower official estimates, these remittances accounted for almost half of Pakistan's total foreign exchange earnings at the time. The Middle East rapidly overtook the UK and Canada as the main source of expatriate Pakistani remittances, soon far exceeding these and foreign aid alike.

The Pakistani economist Omar Noman stressed their significance for the country's economy in a recent study; "By 1984, remittances constituted the largest single source of foreign exchange earnings. They were four times greater than net aid inflow to Pakistan. Not only did they provide 40 per cent of total foreign exchange earnings, but they also financed 86 per cent of the trade deficit".[1]

The seemingly effortless rise in annual remittances until 1983-84 encouraged over-optimism that this bonanza would continue indefinitely. Thus Pakistan's Sixth Five Year Plan (for 1983-88) worked on the false premiss that remittances would grow by ten per cent each year, reaching $4.5 billion in 1988. In fact, remittances declined, because of the numbers of Pakistanis forced to return home with the end of the boom years in the Gulf states.

Official statistics for numbers of Pakistani workers abroad have been vague, or very uncertain, partly because of the undeclared or illegal migrant workers. A 1985 report by the ILO (International Labour Organisation) estimated that in 1983 there were between 1.8 and 2.4 million Pakistanis working in the Middle East region. 59 per cent of these were in Saudi Arabia, with most of the rest in the United Arab Emirates and other small oil-rich Arab states of the Gulf.

The Gulf represents a contemporary 'El Dorado' (the land of Gold), as the Pakistani anthropologist Dr Akbar S. Ahmed commented);

"The saying *Dubai chalo* ' (let us go to Dubai) — which is the equivalent of the expression 'Westward ho' in Western tradition — has become part of

Pakistani culture . . . It signifies the possibility of gathering relatively quick, legitimate, and a great deal of wealth in the Arab states."[2]

Hardly surprisingly the Gulf rapidly became, and still remains, far more important than the earlier places of foreign work or settlement, especially Britain and Canada. Both for individuals and the national economy, there have been obvious benefits.

Gulf remittances made a vital contribution to economic growth in Pakistan through the 1980s. According to some economists, GDP growth was raised from a likely level of around 2 per cent to 5 per cent. The benefits for ordinary people have been spread wide, with an estimated 10 per cent of Pakistani households benefitting by remittances.

Depressed prices for oil on international markets, and the recession in the Gulf economies naturally had a marked impact on Pakistan too, as more workers returned home, and new work opportunities dried up.

What has become steadily more appreciated are the various problems arising out of this remarkable work-migration. One form they take are serious distortions of the Pakistani economy — as is true for those other countries with large numbers of people working in the Gulf, whether Arab or Asian. Most of the money earned by Pakistanis has been spent on imported consumer goods, land and housebuilding, rather than investing in businesses. As little as 10 per cent of the total earnings were being invested productively by returnees from the Gulf, according to a 1982 study by economists based in Lahore.[3]

The very scale of funds flowing back to Pakistan has contributed to high inflation, especially in land values, running at a rate estimated in excess of 20 per cent through much of the 1980s. The rate of inflation in Pakistan is officially placed at around 4 per cent during 1985-87, and considered a matter of pride by the government. However, independent Pakistani economists assess that for lower income groups, the rate of inflation in basic living costs had reached an annual level of between 10 to 15 per cent during that period.

Shortages of skilled men in many fields became common in Pakistani towns. As a direct result, wages have risen sharply. Although the majority of poorer people finding work in the Gulf states have been unskilled labourers — many of them unemployed, or only seasonally employed, at home — there were also many with skills relevant to the construction industry, welding, plumbing, carpentry, etc. Hardly surprisingly, these types of practical vocational skills have since become more highly prized by young men in Pakistan.

At the managerial and professional level, Pakistanis were less numerous in the Gulf than Indians, but proportionately to the pool of available talent, the drain was certainly higher in Pakistan's case. The attraction was not exclusively

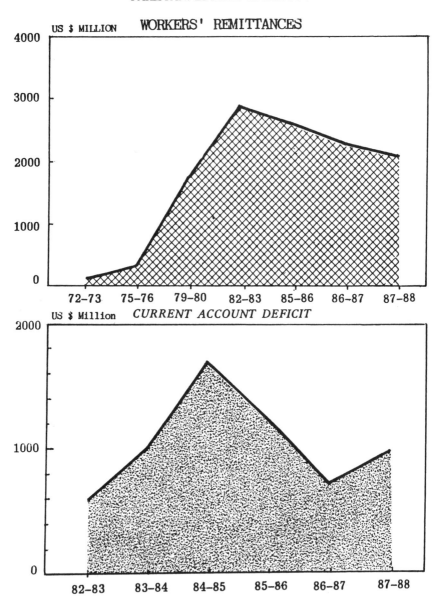

US $ MILLION   WORKERS' REMITTANCES

4000

3000

2000

1000

0

72-73   75-76   79-80   82-83   85-86   86-87   87-88

US $ Million   *CURRENT ACCOUNT DEFICIT*

2000

1000

0

82-83   83-84   84-85   85-86   86-87   87-88

financial. Some exceptionally well qualified Pakistanis went to take posts in the Gulf states in the past decade, not only because of superior salaries and attractive fringe benefits offered, but in quite a few cases because they felt stifled by the political climate in Pakistan.

The drawbacks, however, included some harmful social consequences. They are seen in a spate of medical or psychological symptoms found among a minority of families of the 'guest workers'. The so-called 'Dubai syndrome' undoubtedly stems from the emotional stress caused male workers, their wives and families alike, by coping with new challenges or personal difficulties arising out of separation for many months or even years at a stretch.

Even if many Pakistanis stay for years in the Gulf, and can feel at home in Dubai and other Gulf towns, (where in fact Urdu is very much the lingua franca), they are made well aware that they are aliens in states where foreigners are hired for their usefulness to an Arab ruling class.

One side-effect of the Gulf boom from the 1970s was to make labour supply into one of the most profitable activities in Pakistan. It attracted many greedy and unscrupulous contractors. The lure of the Gulf had unfortunately helped swindlers cheat hundreds of thousands of innocent Pakistanis, from villages and towns, desperate to find well-paid jobs in the oil-rich states of the Gulf. The creation of a special Ministry for Emigrant Workers showed the scale of the problem. Fraud by fake job-recruiting agencies had become so common that in 1979 the military government resorted to setting up military courts to deal with the problem, giving out exemplary punishments to detected swindlers.

THE MILITARY DIMENSION

Pakistan by 1981 had become the second largest supplier of military manpower in the Third World, placed next to Cuba. It had military contingents or missions, large and small, in twenty two countries, with most of them in seven states — Saudi Arabia, the UAE, Oman, Kuwait, Jordan, Syria and Libya.[4] This was, by any standards, a curious combination of states to be linked to in the sensitive area of military aid. It reflected Pakistan's reputation for military competence, as well as earlier links with a variety of type of regime in the Middle East, ranging from ultra-conservative Saudi Arabia to Libya and Syria.

The Gulf region was where Pakistan's military expertise was most in demand, not in carrying on wars like the Cubans in Africa, but in training and internal defence. Technical units of Pakistan's air force and navy as well as the army were serving in Saudi Arabia. Military technicians to help operate sophisticated equipment were being provided by Pakistan in many Gulf states. Pakistani armour and artillery experts, engineers and pilots on contract were particularly numerous in the Gulf states.

In 1983 Saudi Arabia signed two security cooperation agreements, with the emphasis on internal defence for the Kingdom. The naval presence is striking in Saudi Arabia, Oman and the UAE. Besides the hundreds of Pakistani officers and technicians serving in warships and naval establishments in GCC states, Pakistani instructors were also prominent at the new Saudi naval school in Jubail, open to all six Gulf Cooperation Council (GCC) states. A powerful Pakistani naval force visited GCC ports in March 1985, and, according to some reports, a large part of Pakistani naval strength was stationed in Gulf waters from 1985. Karachi itself has the best naval and logistic facilities in the entire Gulf region. New port facilities were being developed at Gwadar and other places along Baluchistan's Makran coast.[5]

Besides the loaning of Pakistani technicians and deployment of units in the Gulf states, officers from Saudi Arabia and other Gulf states are regularly trained in military training institutions in Pakistan itself.

This expanding military role of Pakistan has been the target of fierce criticism by domestic critics, claiming that this development is proof that the 500,000 strong armed forces are simply mercenaries hired out to Arab potentates. The exact numbers of Pakistani troops and advisers stationed abroad in the 1980s is a closely guarded secret. Some published estimates, of a total of 40,000 or even 50,000 Pakistani military personnel serving abroad by 1985 have certainly been exaggerated, but the numbers clearly are large.

It came about, so many critics claim − rather simplistically − because of US pressure on Pakistan to replace Iran as the ''policeman of the Gulf'', after the collapse of the Shah's regime from late 1978. The emergence of the Khomeini regime in Iran in 1979, the seizure of Makka's Great Mosque in 1979 and the beginning of the war between Iran and Iraq all combined to impress the Saudis and other Arab Gulf states with their weakness in defence and security matters.

It was natural for them to turn to Pakistan, since they already enjoyed a close working relationship. And it was natural for the Pakistani military to accept playing a bigger role in return for enhanced financial rewards. Such a policy combined neatly the goals of Pakistan's military rulers with US security priorities in the wider region.

That said, this expanding Pakistani military role in the weaker conservative Arab states of the Gulf clearly did have much to do with the strategic requirements of the US Central Command (Centcom).[5] As American analysts were not slow to point out, by early 1982, the USA and Pakistan appeared ready to renew a defence relationship which had been in a state of suspension ever since 1965.

It was built on the realisation in Washington that Pakistan represented high strategic-military value; "There has long been a propensity in Washington to regard the Pakistani military as first-rate, smart and professional, certainly on any comparative standard . . . Its military is among the few that can effectively assimilate high-technology weapon systems, if only in limited amounts."[6]

The hiring out of military manpower paralled Pakistan's export of manpower in the civil field. Individuals benefit from it by enhanced pay, and at the same time Pakistan's armed forces also gains. As a provider of military personnel to Saudi Arabia, Pakistan gained financially. In addition to large payments for supply of military units, the Saudis reportedly paid for considerable amounts of US weaponry supplied to Pakistan's armed forces in the early 1980s. Not only does this arrangement help generate income to buy weapons, it provides access for Pakistanis to the most sophisticated types of Western military hardware being bought by the GCC states.

Pakistan's military role in the Middle East had, of course, begun much earlier, from the 1950s, in the era of the Baghdad Pact (1955), and its successor organisation the Central Treaty Organisation (CENTO), set up in 1959. Indeed, its antecedents can be traced back to the two World Wars, when the British Indian army played a major part in the fighting throughout the Middle East and North Africa.

Notes

1. Omar Noman, The Political Economy of Pakistan 1947-85. London, KPI, 1988, p 157.
2. Akbar S. Ahmed, Asian Affairs, London, October 1984.
3. see further Omar Noman, ibid, 1988 and Middle East Journal, vol 38, no 4, 1984, Far Eastern Economic Review, Hong Kong, 17 October 1985 and The Middle East Magazine, London, February 1983.
4. Robert G. Wirsing and James M. Roberty, the United States and Pakistan, in International Affairs, London, Autumn 1982.
5. Lawrence Lifschultz in Far Eastern Economic Review, Hong Kong, and Jamal Rashid, Pakistan and the Central Command, in Middle East Report, Washington DC, (July 1986) and Far Eastern Economic Review (Hong Kong), 18 December 1986.
6. quoted from Wirsing and Roberty, ibid, p 593. See also Shirin Tahir-Kheli, The US and Pakistan. The Evolution of an Influence Relationship. Praeger. 1982.

9
Living on Borrowed Time

Pakistan's economy has had an impressive growth rate coupled with a significant rise in real wages over the past decade. Although the economy's general performance has been uneven, it has produced some striking successes, with record crops of cotton, wheat and rice going to fuel an export drive.

Sustained economic growth has averaged almost 7 per cent of GDP since 1979. This remarkable rate has naturally encouraged the government. However, most economists agree that this growth rate cannot be sustained over the long-term without much greater investment. Pakistan's domestic savings are a mere 4.5 per cent of its GDP, as contrasted with India's 20 per cent.[1]

One of the urgent needs for Pakistan is to mobilise (and expand) existing domestic savings for productive purposes. One way this is being attempted is by Islamisation of banking, and various other Islamic measures introduced, in part at least, to overcome the past reluctance by pious Muslims to invest or lend their money through normal commercial banking channels. So far, though, this strategy has had little impact on the level of savings in Pakistan.

A fragile balance of payments position is something which Pakistani planners have long had to live with. But the scale of remittances from Pakistani workers in the Gulf during the 1980s served to relax the country's blance of payments problems, and reduce the trade deficit. The decision in 1982 to make the Pakistani rupee independent of the US$, and its gradual slide in value, helped to make Pakistani exports more price-competitive on world markets.

The Sixth Five-Year Plan (1983-88) specifically set out to solve one of the basic problems − that Pakistan regularly imported about twice as much as it exported. The Plan envisaged a massive concentration of resources on agriculture together with energy development. The Plan also envisaged much larger investment in such neglected sectors as health, rural water supply and basic education. However, many Pakistani economists had early on criticised the Sixth Plan − costed at Rs 490 billion ($33 billion) − as being totally unrealistic, and really tailored to IMF demands rather than to Pakistan's own priorities.

BUDGET DEFICITS

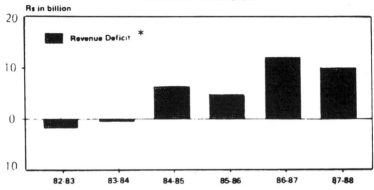

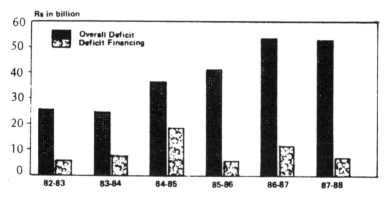

* Bars below zero indicate revenue surplus.

Their criticisms appear to have been largely justified. By the time the civilian government under Prime Minister Junejo came to power in February 1985, this Plan had effectively been scrapped. All of the Plan's targets for spending in these social areas, as in other fields, had fallen far behind, for lack of domestic resources. However, the government's determination to expand exports was further spelled out in June 1987 by the Commerce Ministry, which outlined details of a three-year trade policy, holding out as its goal the doubling of exports by 1990.

Estimates of Pakistan's total receipts of foreign currency placed these at the high figure of some $40 billion in the period 1980-85. They were made up of; export earnings ($15 billion), remittances ($15 billion) and foreign aid ($10 billion). However, the potential benefits of these large sums to help fund the country's development were lost, for the most part, because they went largely to pay for imports of consumer goods, as well as servicing foreign loans, which had grown by 1988 to $14 billion.

Pakistan's economy has been living on borrowed time and borrowed money, according to one of the key architects of the country's financial planning over this period, Dr Mahbubul Haq. Foreign aid and loans regularly financed around one-fifth of the country's annual budget.

The decade 1978-88 has seen non-development expenditure ruse from Rs 25 billion (in 1977-78) to Rs 125 billion in 1987-88. Defence spending rose sixfold in this decade, accounting for between 32 and 38 per cent of total current expenditure. The scale of military spending by Pakistan placed it among the highest in Asia. It is keenly resented by the majority of the public, which appears to believe the generals are pampering the military by buying the best hardware, rather than simply re-equipping the armed forces in dangerous times.

Symptomatic of public feeling was the fate of a highly controversial new defence tax, proposed in the original budget for 1987-88. This took the form of a hefty surcharge on income tax, imports and locally-manufactured goods. Provoking an outcry on all sides, with costly strikes and street demonstrations, the proposed 'defence tax' had to be hastily withdrawn, though in its place some face-saving economy measures were introduced.

For 1988, Pakistan had a record budget deficit of almost Rs 60 billion in a total outlay of less than Rs 200 billion. Although the World Bank and other institutions repeatedly declared that they were deeply concerned over Pakistan's worsening budget deficits, yet the Pakistan Aid Consortium committed aid over recent years at a higher level than anticipated. For 1987-88 the Consortium offered $2.4 billion. Commitments of $2.5 billion for 1988-89 were obtained

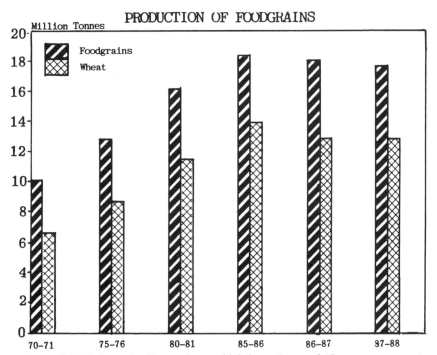

PRODUCTION OF FOODGRAINS

in April 1988 from the Consortium, which is made up of 12 government and nine financial institutions.

The sheer size of Pakistan's budget deficit gave rise to fears in some circles that the country's long-term position would soon become unsustainable. In June 1988, the withholding of a large loan by the World Bank was interpreted by Pakistani analysts as a form of pressure put on the government to finally implement long-requested measures to tackle macroeconomic issues.

Many of the problems of Pakistan's economy are essentially structural. While the savings rate has remained extremely low, Pakistan's taxation base has remained far too narrow to yield sufficient revenues to pay for government programmes. Successive governments have failed to generate sufficient resources to meet spiralling expenditure, particularly in defence and debt-servicing. Pakistan's taxation system contains many anomalies. Direct tax accounted for just Rs 10.2 billion, compared to Rs 42 billion from excise, sales and customs duties, in the fiscal year 1985.

Direct taxes were being paid by just 11,000 companies, with almost three times as many firms left out of account. The failure to tackle the problem of missing revenues had come about through a lack of will on the part of successive governments, unable or unwilling to tackle the resistance of vested interests.

FAVOURED FARMERS

Agricultural income has always been virtually exempt from taxation, although agriculture itself accounts for fully 25 per cent of GDP. The idea of introducing an income tax on agriculture is not new in Pakistan, and since decades, in fact, foreign aid donors have urged it. Under pressure from the World Bank, Pakistan agreed to introduce a selective water tax from mid-1989, over a period of four years. It will be levied on farmers benefiting from new irrigation schemes funded by the World Bank.

Back in 1964, a special land commission backed the proposed tax, but no action followed. Agriculture raises around 18 per cent of indirect taxes.

Taxation on land in Pakistan is such a sensitive issue because it has political implications. The landed lobby has remained very powerful right through Pakistan's history, with members of rich landowning families dominating prliaments. Even the reforming "Socialist" Prime Minister Z.A. Bhutto, (himself, of course, a large landowner, like many other leading lights of the PPP), actually had written into the Constitution of 1973 a special provision excluding agriculture from the income tax mandate of Pakistan's Parliament.

The omission of agricultural income from taxation has also hindered state efforts to obtain tax due from the wealthy business class, many of whom own farms as well as companies. The link is clear, as the Islamabad-based journalist Hussain Haqqani noted in 1987;

"As long as agricultural income remains outside the tax net, assessees can shield income from any other source simply by ascribing it to their farm plots. Most large holdings of land in Pakistan belong to absentee landlords, and even well-off people living in urban areas often show suspiciously profitable farms and gardens on their tax returns".[2]

Tax evasion has been a huge problem, one whose scale was increasingly admitted by a concerned government. There was unanimity that corruption and tax evasion, already endemic in the country, had considerably worsened in the 1980s. As an official report of December 1986 noted, "there is no doubt in the minds of the public that most government and semi-government departments are corrupt".

While the precise extent of corruption can be argued over, its extraordinary spread and growth in the 1980s are beyond doubt. This stems from the influx of money into Pakistan – in particular the vast sums of money available from the booming drugs business which has developed in the 1980s, especially heroin. It is heroin, processed in the Pushtun tribal borderlands since 1980, and smuggled out to the world's markets with connivance from officials of all grades, which fuels corruption. Millions of addicts in Pakistan itself bear witness to the domestic impact of the drugs trade. The heroin culture has spread its insidious effects at all levels of society.

Pakistan's parallel economy may amount to close on one-third of the country's gross national product, according to a 1987 estimate made by the National Taxation Reforms Commission. The Commissions' report, tabled before parliament in Spring 1987, gave the total size of the parallel economy as Rs 180 billion, with the bulk of Pakistan's "black money" apparently held in non-productive investments. These mainly took the form of bank deposits, real estate and undeclared business assets.

The Commission's members denounced the black economy as a self-perpetuating phenomenon, urging drastic measures of prison terms and confiscation of assets for offenders, so to curb its rapid growth. They warned that unless it was checked, "the illegal transactions and black money (will eventually) equal, or perhaps surpass, the legitimate open economy".

Senior Pakistani officials made increasingly blunt complaints from 1987 as to the prevalence of tax evasion, corruption and smuggling. Far stiffer penalities for tax evasion were finally introduced in 1988, together with a radically-restructured tax system.

Dr Mahbubul Haq, as minister for finance, planning and commerce, (and who had previously held other posts of influence on the economy), presented a budget in June 1988 in which important new changes were outlined for Pakistan's taxation laws. The Minister bluntly declared that the country's sick economy, "needs surgery, not more debate". Whether the treatment the doctor recommended constituted surgery, though, was a matter of debate.

The taxation system was both restructured and simplified in the budget, with national tax numbers allotted, while the wide discretionary powers of income tax officers were reduced. The explicit goal of this change was to provide an opportunity for businessmen to pay to the state money which they had been paying to corrupt officials.

If implemented, the budget's proposed changes should result in a reduction of Pakistan's overspending from eight per cent of GDP, under the Junejo government, down to just over five per cent in 1988-89. However, the new tax proposals provoked a vigorous campaign of protest by the business class in cities all over Pakistan, with the threat of national strikes issued by Pakistan's chambers of commerce. The outcome of this dispute was uncertain at the time of writing.

Some of the reforms planned by Dr Mahbubul Haq were on the lines demanded since years by the World Bank and other financial institutions of impeccably orthodox financial views. Others reflected what were claimed to be strictly Islamic values.

There were also moves to introduce a new Value Added Tax, (to be levied on cement and steel), expected to raise Rs 5 billion in 1988-89. This change, resembling the VAT adopted in the EEC states and by many other countries, is something which the World Bank in particular had pressed hard for. A further Rs 8 billion would be raised in 1988-89 from increases in excise and customs duties and income tax.

Recent moves towards disinvestment in state enterprises and state-owned banks seemed to owe their stimulus to the privatisation in Mrs Thatcher's Britain, and to other western experiments to tap domestic resources and private savings for productive investment. The long-awaited offering to the public of shares in 10 per cent of the country's prestigious and profitable Pakistan International Airlines (PIA) was confirmed at the end of 1987. There was less interest in plans to sell off other parts of the ailing public sector. 14 industrial units were set to be privatised in 1988, and 20 per cent of the shares in nationalised banks would be offered for sale.

The Islamic element in this state disinvestment programme consisted of three types of bond-issues to be offered to the Pakistani public, not bearing interest but instead being of the profit-and-loss sharing type. In the same budget were announced a range of financial benefits for middle and lower-income groups, pressed hard by inflation. These benefits were loftily stated to be part of the government's goal to make Islamic justice the cornerstone of economic policy.

The government had aimed at curbing the regular massive budget deficit. However, the annual budget for 1988-89 actually showed an increase in state spending, up by 5.7 per cent, with Defence up by 6.7 per cent.

POPULATION PRESSURES

Pakistan's population growth, at 2.9 per cent annually, is among the world's highest. It deeply worries the country's planners, who see economic progress swallowed up in increasing numbers of extra mouths to feed. With over 100 million people in 1987, Pakistan is the ninth most populous country in the world. Its population will reach at least 150 million by the year 2000, if present trends continue.

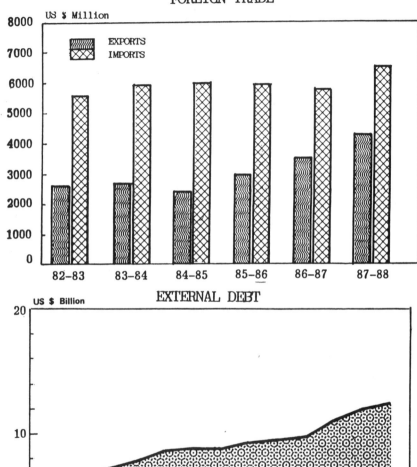

FOREIGN TRADE

EXTERNAL DEBT

It is all the more surprising, then, that family planning in Pakistan lacks firm state backing and encouragement. That causes probably lie in the government's extreme sensitivity to the strident Muslim Fundamentalist circles, which are by and large hostile to contraception and deeply prejudiced against family planning programmes. The problems caused by rapid growth of population are particularly evident in Pakistan's cities. With their facilities already under strain, the crowded towns are set to expand massively through the 1990s. Accounting for 28 per cent of the population by 1986, the cities are likely to hold 44 per cent of some 150 million Pakistanis by the end of the century.

Rapid rural migration to the large cities has caused social and economic dislocation. In the 1980s, the spread of drugs and related activities of so-called "heroin mafias", together with the easy availability of automatic weapons filtered off from the Afghan war, have combined to aggravate existing social tensions, particularly in the case of Karachi, the country's largest city.

Karachi now contains over ten million people in what is the greatest concentration by far of industry, and the country's main port. The breakdown of law and order and acute ethnic tensions among large sections of Karachi's slum-dwellers in 1984-88 became a focus of study and official enquiry. The Karachi disturbances, according to Pakistan's Institute of Policy Studies, were symptoms of a sense of deprivation and frustration which, "may cross the limit of tolerance if the situation is allowed to persist."[3]

SUCCESS IN AGRICULTURE

Outstanding progress in agriculture took place from 1977, in spite of periodic setbacks due to drought conditions and pest infestation, notably in 1983-84. Over the decade as a whole, agriculture was aided by an unusually favourable weather cycle. Pakistan has not only become more or less self-sufficient in wheat and sugar, among its most important crops, it became for the first time a small scale exporter in these too.

The principal cash crop is cotton, followed by rice, for long the largest source of foreign exchange earnings. Records were broken even in the early 1980s for all four main crops – cotton, rice, wheat and sugar-cane – in successive harvests, as a combination of agricultural inputs, insecticides and ideal weather conditions yielded rising productivity. There was an overall agricultural growth rate of 6.5 per cent in 1985-86.

Cotton led the way with a record crop of 7.1 million bales, an increase of 23 per cent. It was due to improved agricultural support services by the government, together with the planting of a new high-yield variety. This was followed by new records of 7.76 million bales (1986-87), and 8.9 million bales (1987-88). The yield of cotton per hectare rose sharply in these years too, from 528 kg to 590 kg. Cotton was a key indicator of the agricultural sector. Booming exports of cotton, cotton-based textiles and clothing together provided a major source of foreign exchange, besides employment for millions of families. In Pakistan farmers call cotton by the name "silver fibre", and it is not only valuable to them as a cash crop. The seed from newly harvested cotton is a prized source of vegetable oil − in short supply in Pakistan. Even that part which remains *(khuli)* after pressing for oil is utilised as animal feed on the farms.

Total production and yield of wheat, Pakistan's main food crop, has gone up satisfactorily in the 1980s, helped by new varieties. Wheat production, centred in the Punjab, increased from 10.9 million tonnes in 1983-84 to 14.2 million tonnes in 1986-87, an annual increase of 7.5 per cent. Over the same period, yield per hectare increased by 27 per cent to 1,880 kg.[4] But bad weather conditions reduced harvests from 1987.

Rice production, especially of high-quality basmati rice, rose from 3.3 million tonnes in 1983-84 to 3.5 million tonnes in 1986-87. For a time in the mid-1980s, Pakistan led as the biggest exporter of rice on world markets. However, Thailand later overtook Pakistan, and in terms both of quality improvement and yield, Pakistan's progress has been only moderate.

Mechanisation has steadily increased since 1973, resulting in shrinking numbers of jobs for farm labourers. One of the current problems being tackled is water-logging and salination, which have reached serious levels in many areas of Punjab and Sind, the two most important agricultural provinces. A plan was prepared in 1986 to combat these dangers, aiming at reclamation of 4.4 million acres of (1.66 million hectares) of land by 1990.

A flourishing agriculture has been the key to Pakistan's success in boosting its exports, up to $4.3 billion in 1987-88, from $3.4 billion in the previous year. However, high international prices for Pakistan's bumper cotton crops may well not last much longer.

Foreign markets for Pakistan's surplus crops were found in many countries. Iran became increasingly important from 1981, as the impact of war began to be felt. Pakistan exported 200,000 tonnes of wheat to Iran in 1984, as well as to Bangladesh. Pakistan became a food lifeline to Iran, providing sugar, wheat, rice, meat, fruit, vegetables and urea fertiliser. In 1984 Iran's purchases of agricultural goods and textiles made it Pakistan's biggest single trading partner, worth in excess of $500 million, paid for mainly in oil. The neglected land route from Pakistan's Baluchistan province became valued as Gulf waters became more perilous for merchant ships, though a part of this trading was conducted by sea. Pakistani hopes of continuing this trade in the long-term, even after the conclusion of a negotiated peace between Iran and Iraq, seem to be realistic. Iran was reportedly negotiating a five-year barter agreement swapping oil for rice, which could treble the value of two-way trade between the two countries. Iran committed itself in 1988 to back plans to develop new port and road facilities in Pakistan, so as to facilitate bulk trade between the two neighbour states.

Pakistan has recently developed barter and counter-trade deals with countries of Eastern Europe, Asia and Africa too. The government's new insistence on trading partners with large credit balances taking a minimum proportion of goods from Pakistan helped increase exports. Imported edible oils formed a major item of barter. Parkistan's imports of various types of edible oils totalled 864,000 tonnes in 1985-86, costing $294 million. Demand rises by 13 per cent each year for Pakistan's state-subsidised edible oil.

PROBLEMS WITH ENERGY

State schemes to develop the energy sector and infrastructure have failed to keep pace with the rapid increase in industrial and domestic demand. Shortages of energy were blamed on failure to make adequate investment in badly-needed infrastructure for generating electricity and other forms of energy.

Pakistan's industrial progress has been severely handicapped by inadequate infrastructure. Power shortages in the cities made load-shedding very common at peak periods of demand for electricity. An ambitious scheme for hydroelectric power has been blocked for years because of inter-provincial rows and shortage of finance. This is the Kalabagh Dam, to be constructed on the Indus river downstream from the existing Tarbela dam.

The extension of electricity supply to remote villages took place at an accelerating rate from 1980. In the four provinces, a claimed 3405 villages were connected to the national grid in the year 1986-87 alone, as contrasted with the total of 9,560 villages electrified in the 20-year period 1959-1980.

Production of natural gas, centred in Baluchistan, expanded with new discoveries. Production of natural gas rose to 402.6 billion cu ft in 1986-87. Gas and electricity together accounted for 76 per cent of total energy consumed by industry in 1983, but this pattern changed from mid-1980s. Changes in the government's policy of holding down gas prices led to increasing substitution (for example, by the cement industry) in the use of fuelds, in favour of oil and coal.

A succession of promising new discoveries of natural gas, oil and coal deposits from 1984 revived optimism in the energy sector, after many disappointments in prospecting Pakistan's complex geological structures.

Pakistan had regularly imported oil and petroleum products to a value of around $1.5 billion in the early 1980s − the country's major import item. But as a result of new oil discoveries, all small so far, Pakistan's domestic oil production rose steadily from 1985, reaching 48,000 b/d by March 1988. One-third of Pakistan's crude oil requirement was being met by domestic sources in 1988.

An oil exploration programme has expanded since 1984, led by thirteen companies − nine of them foreign. There were high hopes for offshore oil exploration, with oil rigs being supplied by Canada and the USSR.

The steel mill at Pipri, near Karachi, is the country's largest industrial complex, employing 19,000 people. It is a rare example of Soviet-Pakistani collaboration, and 800 Soviet engineers and technicians were still working there in 1984. There was anticipation in Pakistan that the USSR might unilaterally end its part in this large project, over a period of acute tension caused by Soviet opposed interests to Pakistan's Afghan policy.

Taking almost a decade to bring into production finally in 1984, the steel mill has often been criticised as a white elephant which can never hope to break even, absorbing moreover an unhealthily large part of state investment resources. The project had originally been agreed under Bhutto, and Pakistan's engineering industry is expected to benefit eventually from it by many downstream projects. Beset by many problems and high costs, nevertheless Pakistan Steel claimed that the Pipri mill was saving $150 million annually in imports from abroad.

One of Pakistan's most crisis-ridden industries in the 1980s has been carpets. Until 1980 this sector ranked third in export earnings, after cotton products and rice. Most of the 40 million sq ft of carpets and rugs produced each year were exported, mainly to EEC states, earning $172 million in 1983-84. In 1985 the Carpet Export Promotion Committee of Pakistan claimed that half the country's looms were closed, and one million jobs threatened.

Private investment in large- and medium-scale manufacturing industry was weak over the decade from 1977, in spite of various incentives offered by the government, whose strategy for industrial growth really depended upon participation by private entrepreneurs. Political uncertainty was a factor which weighed against industrial investments, at least in the early years of Zia's rule.

One basic cause of the disappointing response, though, were the unrivalled financial returns (and excellent investment prospects for the future) offered by investing in real estate in Karachi and other cities in Pakistan in this period.[5]

Housebuilding in Pakistan, as elsewhere, offered spectacular returns, thanks to inflation and high demand, without the risks involved in business ventures.

Notes: The Economy

1. Omar Noman, The Political Economy of Pakistan 1947-85, KPI, London 1988. p 146.
2. Far Eastern Economic Review, Hong Kong, 19 March 1987.
3. quoted from Pakistan chapter of The Asia & Pacific Review 1988, Saffron Walden, Essex, UK, 1988.
4. Economic Survey 1987-88, Government of Pakistan, Finance Division, Islamabad, 1988.
5. see further in Omar Noman, 1988, ibid, part three, chapter 3 (Economic Developments).

President (General) Zia-ul-Haq with the Prime Minister of India Mr. Rajiv Gandhi, on December 17, 1985 — just before the Indo-Pak official talks began in New Delhi.
Photo: Courtesy India House.

10
Zia: A Troubled Legacy

Within days of General Zia's death the caretaker government of Pakistan was forced to issue denials that martial law had been reimposed following a wave of strong rumours that the army had staged another coup. This was, of course, a false alarm. What had really happened was that three of the four provincial chief ministers had met the new chief of the army staff, General Aslam Baig and reportedly suggested to him that the return of martial law would be preferable to free elections in which Pakistan People's Party (PPP) led by Benazir Bhutto might win. General Baig, at least for the time being, politely rejected their demand. This meeting, however, between the army chief and three of Zia's most trusted lieutenants was enough to spread rumours amongst the apprehensive people of Pakistan that the military was going to deny them the promised elections.

We do not know yet the real intentions of the military establishment in Pakistan but this incident explains the psyche of the people in that country. The fact that all the important political leaders of Pakistan (including Benazir Bhutto) carefully avoided the direct criticism of the army after Zia's death is further explanation of the psyche. It must be remembered that the much acclaimed 'constitutional' transition of power, took place soon after the General's death, was actually a decision taken by the military itself who decided to make Ghulam Ishaq Khan, the Senate Chairman, as acting President. All three previous coups in Pakistan had been carefully planned in advance, and the only time power was really handed over to an elected leader was in 1972, when after the crushing defeat in a war with India which resulted in dismemberment of the country, Chairman of the PPP, Zulfikar Ali Bhutto was given charge of the demoralized nation.

Field Marshal Mr Sam Manekshaw, the celebrated former army chief in India (architect of Indian victory in 1971) was recently asked in a BBC interview:[1] "Why have there been so many coups in Pakistan and Bangladesh, but not a single one in India, despite the fact that Generals in all three countries have come from similar backgrounds and training by the British who had always taught them to take orders from the elected politicians''. Manekshaw was quick in his answer. He said, ''Because in India the politicians have looked after their country quite well while their counterparts in neighbouring Pakistan and Bangladesh failed in their duty in this regard.''

Surprisingly, Manekshaw's answer is similar to that given by Generals in Pakistan and Bangladesh, blaming the politicians for all the failures. However, in the case of Pakistan this appears to be largely true. Bhutto, in particular, is blamed for losing an historic opportunity to lay the firm democratic foundations in the country and cut the military down to size for good. He came to power, says the argument, when the military had lost its power, its prestige and its morale. He could have created a wider political base for his party and generated a healthy democratic environment in the country as a whole and should not have allowed, as he did, the military to regain political strength by deploying it in Baluchistan and other areas to crush the popular dissent.

This argument is only partly true. First of all, by his background and temperament Bhutto was not a democrat. He was essentially a populist politician who with his emotional speeches and slogans could raise the aspirations amongst people which he apparently could not satisfy, as explained in an earlier chapter. Furthermore, his popularity to a large extent was due to the failures of military regimes (though ironically he himself was involved with both Ayub and Yahya regimes), and the disunity amongst other political parties. Secondly, his decision to send the army in to Baluchistan was taken partly on pressure from the Shah of Iran, who was concerned about the implications of Baluchi nationalism in his own country which had a sizeable Baluchi population bordering Pakistan.

But the most important factor overlooked in this analysis is the army itself. In Pakistan, the military is the only organised institution in the country which has grown in strength, power and base over the years. It has taken care of itself very well in Pakistan's 41-year troubled history. After the 1971 debacle it had carefully reorganised itself, regained strength and confidence and, then, just waited for the opportune time to come. And when the time came, as it did in 1977, the army jumped in and took over the reigns of power. It must also be remembered that army is the most powerful institution in Pakistan. As many writers have already pointed out, even after long four decades the search for a nation is still not over in Pakistan. It was clear after the birth of Bangladesh in 1971 that Islam alone could not bind Pakistan together. There has to be a basis on which people from all the remaining four provinces could feel equal partners in the process of nation building. Bhutto failed as he decided against continuing this process, started with the 1973 constitution, because ultimately he could not see power beyond himself. And General Zia failed because it threatened his very base, what he proudly used to call − 'my only constituency' i.e. army.

Indeed, General Zia throughout his eleven years nourished his own constituency. As a representative of the army the trauma of defeat in 1971 must have been stuck in his mind. Equally important would have been the thought of the popular base of Bhutto. He saw to it that these two problems should not threaten the Pakistani military establishment in future. He carefully avoided another fullfledged war with India while at the same time continued with a nuclear programme at home. He put Bhutto on trial and ensured that his execution go ahead. No doubt the most important service he did to his constituency was to re-establish the military as the most powerful political institution in the country. This is Zia's main legacy. His Islamization programme at home and support for the Afghan Mujahideen at the foreign policy level were two powerful means to achieve the end of his primary goal.

IMAGE AND REALITY

Zia successfully created for himself an image as a pious and devout Muslim. Though we do not question the sincerity of his personal belief, his type of Islam created fear even among the deeply religious people of Pakistan. Zia also managed to attain a reputation for himself as an honest man, despite the fact that he developed a habit of dishonouring his own promises − earning him a variation of his official title CMLA (not 'Chief Martial Law Administrator' but 'Cancel My Last Announcement'). He also fostered his image as a very friendly, direct and simple man unlike a typical military dictator. But his actions proved he was very much a military dictator, and as to his friendly nature, even his "friends" could never predict what his next move would be. He is known as the most stable Pakistani ruler, though actually this stability was a temporary phenomenon based on the longest period of continued martial law in his country's history, and on the Afghan factor. As 'The Times' of London wrote: "Unfortunately, Pakistan is still no more stable than when he came to power. That is his failure."[2] In the same manner his economic "achievements" were also shallow, based almost entirely on foreign factors (aid and Gulf remittances) and illegal drug trafficking.

Zia's prominant characteristic, which is not disputed, is political astuteness. This was certainly rare for someone of his background. Throughout his eleven years he successfully fought off the forces which would or could have destabilized him. It is doubtful whether the Pakistani military could ever find another General with political and diplomatic skills which could match those of Zia-ul-Haq. Even the most seasoned politicians at times looked like beginners beside him. All other previous military rulers in Pakistan were known to be used by the West for its own interests. General Zia, however, appeared to use the west for his own interests. Although the Afghanistan factor was mainly responsible for this, it is inconceivable to imagine a Pakistani politician or General other than Zia managing to extract such a large amount of aid and political support from the West without any real strictures, despite the continued reports of human rights violations (alleged by Amnesty International and Pakistani opposition) in the country, an uninterrupted programme to make the nuclear bomb and government's inability (if not the lack of will) to control illegal drug trafficking − for which the victims included people in the west.

Although General Zia's political skills and astuteness grew with time, he showed signs of this shrewdness soon after he came to power. On the one hand he started discrediting and weakening the political leaders and on the other, by pressing through a programme of Islamization, he effectively used Islam to distract peoples' attention from the economic and political issues. And he continued throughout his regime with a combination of these two points to change the political map of Pakistan and to institutionalize the role of military in its political life. Unlike his follower General Ershad in Bangladesh, he did not have to press for this role before the politicians. His skills, actions and, of course, the circumstances allowed him to do so openly and with a considerable degree of coolness.

SOLDIER OF ISLAM

Zia was well aware of the fact that the name of Islam was very dear to the hearts of the Pakistani people. The country was created on this basis, though no Pakistani leader before him attempted to enforce such a vigorous programme of Islamization Zia tried to make people in and outside Pakistan believe that the root cause of the country's problems was failure in this regard. In August 1977 he told the nation: . . . "had the Islamic system been introduced at the appropriate time all basic necessities of every citizen would have been met easily . . .". And explaining to Indian journalist and writer M.J. Akbar, Zia said: ". . . This country was created in the name of Islam. And the moment that sight was lost, what remained? You take away the ideology of an ideological state, nothing is left. And this is why Pakistan faced hurdle after hurdle: the identity was not established. The basic philosophy was lost and people were groping in the dark . . . that is why we have been unfortunate. You had your goal set, and went off on that way. This is why we find that India is well set while Pakistan is still groping."[3]

106

But Zia also knew that the people of Pakistan, in spite of their deep religious belief, do not want the state to impose islamization from above as they regard religious faith to be their personal matter. They had earlier proved this by rejecting the fundamentalist parties in every available election opportunity they were given. The very low turn-out in Zia's referendum on his Islamization programme in December 1984 also underlined the same point. The unilateral declaration of Islamization was seen by his critics as simply one of his strategies to legitimise his rule. Islamization wa also used as one of the main weapons to crush the opposition. Political workers and journalists critical of the army regime were given flogging sentences. This Islamization programme was used to justify the holding of non-party-based elections. Indeed, Zia himself was quoted on several occasions as saying that under the Islamic system a woman could not be head of the state − a clear reference to Benazir Bhutto.

The Islamization programme also meant the enhancement of status of Maulvis (the muslim clergy) in every day life. Their frequent appearances on national Television and influence in the selection of programmes was widely felt by the viewers. But even more important was their increased role in the armed forces.[4] Zia saw to it that in the military, particularly the younger officers and recruits, should strictly follow the religious belief. In early 1978 while addressing the graduates at the officers' training academy at Kakul, General Zia emphasised their role as the "guardians of ideological as well as geographical frontiers."[5] During his rule Zia's association with the fundamentalist Jamaat-i-Islami party was quite close, though in later years this alliance did not remain that strong when the Jamaat criticised General Zia many times.

This programme also created bitter divisions in the social strata of Pakistan. Women vehemently opposed the Islamic measures which made them inferior in society. Pakistani women's groups were particularly opposed to a law passed in 1984 which stipulated that the testimony of two women was equal to one man's on certain cases. Apart from women, Pakistan's 15 percent strong Shia minority community also opposed the Islamization which they saw as the imposition of Sunni Islam on them. Another sect, the Ahmedia community, also felt persecuted when in April 1986 an ordinance prescribed prison sentences for Ahmedis who refered to themselves as Muslims, or who antagonised other Muslims by their behaviour. It must be said, though, the persecution of Ahmedias has been a continuing process in Pakistan. Even the 'liberal' government of Bhutto declared Ahmedis to be a non-muslim sect.

The general impact of Islamization was, however, what Zia had aimed at. It succeeded in initiating a major debate and discussion inside Pakistan, diverting people's attention from political issues. It also gave the military a new weapon to justify its rule. But this programme is likely to have far reaching implications for the future political history of Pakistan. That is why many people in Pakistan now believe the programme of Islamization is going to remain, with possibly some minor amendments, no matter who stays in power in Islamabad.

ADAPTING THE EXISTING INSTITUTIONS:

General Zia also succeeded in his aim of destroying the political parties of his country to a large extent. His astute role in dividing the political parties against each other was first evident at the time of the Bhutto trial. Throughout the trial he kept promising PPP's opponents that fresh elections were going to take place soon. Some of these leaders even accepted government posts in Zia's 1978 cabinet. During the same period political leaders from NWFP and Baluchistan province were released. It helped Zia to gain their support for the Bhutto trial and eventual hanging. But soon after the hanging, which failed to create a mass revolt in Pakistan, he tightened his grip on political leaders by widespread arrests, banning all political parties and political activity and imposing strict press censorship. Continued military rule forced many political leaders to leave the country. All these factors combined to make powerful dents in the organisation of all the political parties. However, Zia could not affect the political aspirations of the people who quite clearly showed their enthusiasm during the elections in 1985 with a heavy turn out. They further demonstrated this in their sincere and widespread support to Benazir Bhutto when she returned home in 1986. This expression was not limited to their support to Bhutto or any political activity, it was also an expression of rejection to the Zia regime.

Two other institutions which suffered under General Zia were the civil service and judiciary. The Civil service or bureaucracy as it is more appropriately called was co-ruler of Pakistan with the military until 1971. Its importance started deteriorating under Bhutto, who used to take all the decisions himself and run both his party and the country as his own estate. He used bureaucracy for his own political purposes and also put his own men from PPP in top civil positions. Although the bureaucracy under Zia did regain to a large extent its strength, the military had the upper hand.

General Zia infiltrated the civil service with people from the military. Many top civilian posts were filled by military officers. He created many new civilian posts for army men. It helped him remove some potential 'trouble makers' from the army on one hand, and rewarded some loyal officers on the other. Many such officers were given ambassadors' jobs abroad. In 1982, 43 per cent of all Pakistan's ambassadors came from the military.[6] The replacement of the bureaucracy by the military was another example of strengthening the institutional role of the military in Pakistan's life.

The Judiciary suffered a great deal during the eleven years. It must be admitted that Pakistan's judiciary, in general, does not have a very high reputation since it accepted the martial law regime of Ayub Khan in 1958.[7] But there have always been exceptions when some courts stayed the sentences passed by a military court. Some judges even dared to declare that a specific government order was illegal.[8] However, the Zia regime ensured with the help of many 'Constitutional' orders that even exceptions could not occur. This was after and in spite of the fact that the Pakistani judiciary largely co-operated with the Zia regime exceptionally well.

The Supreme Court invoking the 'doctrine of necessity' in its judgement on Zia's army coup, said on November 10, 1977: "The new regime represents not a new legal order but only a phase of constitutional deviation dictated by necessity". It added ". . . the court would like to state in clear terms that it has found it possible to validate the extra-constitutional ction of the chief martial law administrator not only for the reason that he stepped in to save the country at a time of a grave national crisis . . . but also because of the solemn pledge given him that the period of constitutional deviation shall be of as short a duration as possible and that during this period all his energies shall be directed towards creating conditions conducive to the holding of free and fair elections leading to the restoration of democratic rule in accordance to the dictates of the constitution."

Although this judicial justification of Zia's coup was disliked and criticised by the supporters of PPP and many others inside and outside Pakistan, a large number of people in Pakistan welcomed it, since the court granted Zia only a conditional reprieve. However, as later events were to show, Zia cunningly ignored the conditional part of the judgement. The Supreme court also upheld the death sentence on Bhutto passed earlier by the Punjab High Court. It is interesting to note that the seven member bench of Pakistan Supreme contained four Punjabi and three non-Punjabi judges, with all Punjabi judges finding him guilty and all three non-Punjabis acquitting him. Zia obviously did not like the dissenting decision of the three judges. Soon after Bhutto was hanged, he frequently used military courts to try people charged with offences under martial law. Later these military courts were given more powers than the civilian courts.

Then, in March 1980 Zia issued a Provisional Constitutional Order which took away the rights of civilian courts to review any politically important executive action, and declared all court decisions void on the legality of martial law." Another important point in this Constitutional Order was to give the

TOTAL EXPENDITURE ON HEALTH
(At Current Prices)

(Rs million)

Year	Development Expenditure	Non-Development Expenditure	Total Expenditure	GNP	Total Expenditure % GNP
1977-78	512.00	558.60	1070.60	172,064	0.62
1978-79	569.00	641.60	1210.60	192,571	0.63
1979-80	717.00	661.89	1378.89	228,886	0.60
1980-81	942.00	794.82	1736.82	270,288	0.64
1981-82	1037.00	993.10	2030.10	315,183	0.64
1982-83	1183.00	1207.00	2390.00	365,585	0.65
1983-84	1526.00	1564.90	3090.90	412,343	0.75
1984-85	1587.45	1785.12	3372.57	469,200	0.72
1985-86	1881.51	2393.81	4275.32	526,569	0.81
1986-87	2615.00	3270.00	5885.00	573,146	1.03
1987-88	3114.41	3600.00	6714.41	610,400	1.10
Sixth Plan Total	10724.37	12613.83	23338.20	2591,658	0.90

Source: Finance Division. Government of Pakistan.

executive powers to dismiss judges. This order, however, was not accepted by all the members of the judiciary outrightly. 19 Supreme Court and provincial High Court judges declined to endorse this 'Constitutional Order', and as a result lost their positions. There were many lawyers who also protested this order. They were arrested under martial law regulations.

But we must repeat these were the exceptions. The military regime succeeded to a large extent in taming the judiciary and, therefore, in eroding its credibility and strength. Even after the lifting of martial law attempts continued to subjugate the judiciary. Zia's latest attempt in this regard was the introduction of Shariah ordinance only two months before his fatal crash and death. This ordinance allowed the country's highest religious court to examine the validity of all laws in terms of how they conform to Islamic beliefs. For many Pakistanis this was yet another vindication of their fears about the military-mullah alliance.

ECONOMY:

Pakistan under President Zia attained a high rate of growth. But this was not the result of any real economic vision or a farsighted policy. The economic prosperity seen during the Zia years was superficial, as it was largely based on substantial foreign aid, record remittances from expatriate Pakistanis in the Gulf and illicit earnings from drugs and guns trade that also flourished during these years. Indeed, many progressive and redistribution policies started by Bhutto regime were reversed. The most important decision was to reverse the policy of nationalization. He also repealed the Land reforms of the Bhutto government announced in 1977. Pakistan Government's own economic survey for 1987-88 admitted that income distribution, both rural and urban, had worsened, even compared to the days in the 1960s when Pakistan's top 22 families controlled two-thirds of the country's wealth.

Defence continued to take the lion's share in successive budgets at the cost of expenditure on development. For instance, Zia's last budget, announced in June 1988 provided Rs48.31 bn for defence (the single largest item of expenditure) whereas the total money provided for all development projects was Rs.47.14bn. Moreover, actual spending on development has been even less. During the last five year plan (1983-88), actual government spending on development came to around Rs250bn against its target of Rs350bn. The Zia government's record in other priority areas also remained dismal. Omar Noman, author of 'Political Economy of Pakistan' (KPI London) has calculated that between 1976-77 to 1982-83 the share of expenditure on education fell from 2.1 per cent of GNP to 1.5 per cent. Similarly World Bank's 'World Development Report' of 1984 said that only five countries in the world spend less than Pakistan on health. These figures indicate that the Zia regime lost a historic opportunity to invest money in the long term development of Pakistan. No government in Pakistan had so much money at its disposal in the past, coupled with the minimum rate of unemployment, as Zia regime did. This money could have been used to correct the regional imbalance and disparities. Instead, it was used to fatten the already privileged armed forces and on the imports of large amounts of consumer goods.

The Bhutto Government had not attempted to correct the regional disparities in the whole of the country. But it did at least correct some past discrimination against the Sindhis, largely because Bhutto himself was a Gindhi and his party PPP had the largest number of supporters there. During his regime Sindhis were equally treated with Punjabis. In some cases they were even given preference. The other two provinces continued to suffer in terms of economic development vis-a-vis the Punjab and Sind, though, Pathans had their share in the armed forces and their large presence in Karachi, controlling the private transport sector.

Zia once again brought back the dominance of Punjabis even over the heads of Sindhis. Many Sindhis appointed in influential positions by Bhutto were dismissed . Sindhis were more agitated and disturbed by the decision of Zia to allot large plots of lands to retired Punjabi military officers. Some of this land was the best in Sind. Many loyal bureaucrats of the military also benefited in these and allottments. This resentment was an important reason of support to anti-government MRD agitation in Sind in 1983.

The prosperity which came to North West Frontier Province mainly as a result of the Afghan problem helped avoid any revolt against the military rule, though, in terms of development this region remained as underdeveloped as ever. In Baluchistan, however, the Zia regime started many development projects. But this does not appear to be an exercise in correcting the regional disparities and removing the grievances of the Baluchi people. The Baluchis continued to be largely excluded from the armed forces and other positions of importance in Pakistan. Even in their own province most of the top positions were filled by either ex-military men or other loyalists from Punjab.

Although Zia's strategy in dealing with Baluchistan differed from that of Bhutto which was based on confrontation, many critics have questioned Zia's real motives behind the development projects. They say that most of the infrastructure development was aimed at increasing the mobility of the army in the hitherto hostile but strategically important terrain of Baluchistan. The other objective is economic. During the last 41 years of Pakistan, most of the rich mineral resources remained unexploited in Baluchistan. The increased presence of many industrial houses from other parts of Pakistan in the province during the Zia years has also worried the Baluchi leaders, as it reminded them of the economic exploitation of erstwhile East Pakistan during the 1950s and 1960s by the industrialists of West Pakistan.

However, Baluch leaders remained bitterly divided during the Zia years on throwing up any effective challenge to the government. Zia succeeded in luring many 'Sardars' (tribal leaders) to become shareholders in his development programme in the province. Zia's apparent conciliatory approach to them had also played its part. It must also be noted that the ordinary Baluch suffered and became tired from the continued armed confrontation of Baluchi nationalists with the army under Bhutto. In this respect the Zia years gave the Baluchis not only relief but also hopes for an upliftment in their economic standards through the development programme. But even Zia did not appear to make any attempt to tackle the political grievances. Thus, we do not think Zia left a legacy of long term stability even in Baluchistan.

AFGHANISTAN

Now we come to the Afghanistan factor which we believe was not itself a legacy of President Zia but the important means to achieve his overall goal i.e. to re-establish the military as the main political institution in Pakistan, which, as we said earlier, is Zia's real legacy. There is no doubt that the handling of the Afghan question by Zia was an important factor behind the Soviet Union's decision of eventual withdrawal of troops from Afghanistan. We do not, however, agree with the former U.S. national security adviser Zbigniew Brezenzinski, who has tried to lead us to believe in his tributes to Zia that he was "the architect of the Soviet Union's greatest political and military defeat.

It is almost music to the western ear to hear that Zia acted as a bulwark against the Soviet Union and communist expansionism, or as a supporter of the freedom fighters in Afghanistan. The truth is that Zia acted in his own interest, which was partly also the interest of Pakistan. He certainly could not have ignored the presence of a superpower, by and large hostile to Pakistan, at his very doorstep. That was also a time when he needed an important external factor to rescue his regime from a threat of growing opposition at home and the unfavourable attitude of most of the world towards him. The economy was beset by problems, western aid had been cut right back, tension was increasing and, of course, the threat of another coup by his fellow army officers was always there. The risk of another war with India would have been too risky.

In these circumstances, the Soviet intervention in the Afghanistan problem came as a welcoming boon for Zia. The new geo-political situation was such that he did not have to ask the U.S. for help. It came without much of his effort. The only thing he had to do was to use his diplomatic skills and determination to bargain the best possible deal, which he successfully did, for his 'services'. This deal was not limited to providing Pakistan with billions of military and economic aid, as the world realized later. Zia also managed to get the United States's muted forgiveness for most of his repressive actions at home. Support for Afghan mujahideen came at the cost of heavy sufferings by Pakistanis. Thus, the real price for the Afghan deal was paid by the people of Pakistan.

Zia's continued martial law for eight years, his repression of political and other opposition and even his alleged programme of nuclear Bomb was largely ignored by the U.S. administration. Even in the west, many people question the judgement of their governments over their apparent silence over General Zia's Islamization measures, under which frequent violations of human rights were widely reported by the world media. Similar measures in Iran, people recalled, attracted harsh criticism by these governments.

For the people of Pakistan, the Afghan problem brought side effects that created big dents in the social fabric. The easy availability of guns and drugs affected the society so much that the real implications go beyond Zia period. It was widely believed that a big portion of all the weapons supplied to Afghan mujahideen fighters reached in the private markets all over Pakistan. Pakistani officials have been quoted in April 1988 as saying that up to half the arms from the US and elsewhere intended for the Afghan Mujahiden forces are siphoned off in Pakistan or are sold back into the country by the Mujahideen. These officials also estimated the country's illegal stock of Kalashnikov rifles at 135,000.[12]

Furthermore, many skilled gunsmiths in Pakistan have been able to make copies of these imported guns, which has increased the supply of arms in the market on one hand, and cut their prices on the other. This factor has brought the price of arms within the reach of a very large number of Pakistanis. Arms Bazaars of Darra Adam Khel (near Peshawar) and Karachi have attained international publicity. The easy availability of these arms has also, naturally, increased their use. In the ethnic riots of Karachi and other places in recent years, these arms have been freely used, resulting in the dangerous expansion of the law and order problem. These arms have also reportedly reached India across the border coming into the hands of the Sikh extremists, and increasing tension between the two governments.

A substantial increase in easy availability and smuggling of drugs is another offspring of the Afghan problem. Indeed, this is known as Zia's other legacy. Pakistan under Zia achieved the status of the world's biggest exporter of heroin.[13] The opium poppies are grown on the bordering areas of North West Frontier Province with Afghanistan. Thanks to the Afghan war, Pakistan was producing 800 tonnes of opium a year, which made 80 tonnes of heroin. The heroin addition has also affected a large number of people in Pakistan. The official figures say it has reached to the order of 800,000, which is nearly three and a half per cent of the adult male population![14] Zia government failed to curb this problem despite U.S. pressures partly because a large number of senior army officers and other influential people in Pakistan are believed to be involved in the drugs trade.

The presence of three million Afghan refugees has also created problems in Pakistani society. Despite the Geneva agreement, many people in Pakistan believe these refugees will never go back. Indeed, a large number of them are already settled in business and other jobs. Some of the Mujahideen leaders have used U.S. aid money to set up businesses and for buying properties in Pakistan.[15] Their enviable life style has also created tensions. Then, infighting between various guerilla groups and activities of Afghan secret service KHAD have directly affected the host population. Zia was well aware of these side effects of the Afghanistan problem. But he apparently did not feel personally threatened by them. Divisions and infighting amongst the Afghan guerilla leaders helped him in maintaining a more effective control over them. The lawlessness created as a result of the gun trade and the drug trafficking were indirectly helping the military. The blame for these problems could easily be given to the Afghan issue, while at the same time justifying the continued military control over the country. As mentioned earlier, many army officers were allegedly involved in the drug trade. It suited Zia that as many army officers as possible could share the 'fruits' of power. The Afghan factor also helped him in altering the ethnic balance in Baluchistan, where a large number of Afghan refugees were settled, making the Pushtun population more than ever dominant there. It significantly reduced the strength of dissident Baluchis. On the other hand, in the North West Frontier Province the existing political issues were comfortably overshadowed by the Afghan war.

Under these circumstances it is not altogether surprising that Zia wanted to continue with the Afghan war, inspite of the agreement reached at Geneva. We also think that while doing so he was not really helping the United States or the West in general. He always encouraged the more fundamentalist groups headed by Gubuddin Hekmatyar's Hezbi-i-Islami party, much to the dislike of the West. He realized that a fundamentalist government in Kabul would be more dependent on Pakistan in future than a moderate democratic government, since the fundamentalist regime would be weaker in its popular support inside Afghanistan. Secondly, this government would justify his own Islamization policy at home. In this decision his rivalry with neighbouring India was also occupying his mind. A fundamentalist government would be abhored by New Delhi as it could give Islamabad a leverage over relations with Afghanistan. With such a regime in Kabul, the West would also be more dependent on Pakistan.

It is also widely believed that under Zia the United States became more unpopular in Pakistan than it ever was. Many Pakistanis blame the United States for their sufferings during the last eleven years, which were either as a direct result of the military government's repressive policies or from the side effects of the Afghan problem. It should be remembered that the most violent anti-American demonstrations ever held in Pakistan were under Zia in November 1979, when mobs of Pakistani youths attacked the U.S. embassy in Islamabad and other American buildings in Pakistani cities. And it was also Zia who took his country out from the western defence pact CENTO, and joined the Non-Aligned movement.

Of course, all this was before the Soviet intervention in Afghanistan and at a time when the U.S. relations with Pakistan, even at the official level, were at a low ebb. The Afghanistan factor did not help much in the improvement of the American image with the Pakistani people. This image, in fact, further deteriorated. The anti-American slogans were heard throughout the Zia years in Pakistan at various protest marches and meetings. As late as June 1988 a women's march organised by the 'Women's Action Forum' protesting against Zia's Islamization was seen in Lahore with slogans including "We don't want American Islam".[16] Such anti-American feelings must be very frustrating for the United States, which has poured billions of dollars of aid into Pakistan during these years.

We do not mean, of course, that the United States and the West did not benefit from President Zia. He will be remembered as a friend and ardent supporter of the Afghan mujahideen, and for his key role in forcing the Soviets out of Afghanistan. He certainly helped the West in pursuance of its strategic policy in Southern and Western Asia (the Middle East). His close relationship with the conservative Islamic World was also helpful to Western interests, particularly after the fall of the Shah in Iran. But unlike his predecessors in Pakistan, the military regime of Zia successfully maintained a relationship with the West, based on give and take, though he, of course, was a junior partner in this relationship. As a hard bargainer he never gave anything away without charging a heavy price.

Many Pakistanis suffered under his rule. But who cares? He was after all a military dictator who never claimed that he was a politician! It is another matter that he was more astute as a diplomat than many professional politicians in Pakistan and, indeed, elsewhere. History will remember General Zia more as a shrewd diplomat, a wily politician and a master of public relations skills than as a tyrant and military dictator. However, Pakistanis might simply remember him as a cunning general who moulded their country and their institutions to the extent that after his death they could not imagine Pakistan free from military control.

Notes

1. In an interview with Naresh Kaushik for BBC Hindi Service broadcast on August 24, 1987.
2. The Times, London August 18, 1988.
3. Akbar, M.J. "India: The Siege Within", Penguin Books, London 1985.

4. Noman, Omar, "The Political Economy of Pakistan 1947-85", KPI Limited, London 1988.
5. Pakistan Times, April 14, 1978.
6. Rizvi, H.A., "Paradox of Military Rule in Pakistan", Asian Survey, May, 1984.
7. Ali, Tariq, "Can Pakistan Survive", Penguin Books, London 1988.
8. Noman, Omar, "The Political Economy of Pakistan 1947-85", KPI Limited, London.
9. Ibid.
10. Haqqani, Hussain, Far Eastern Economic Review, March 3, 1988.
11. The Times, London August 26, 1988.
12. Quoted in the Financial Times, London April 7, 1988.
13. The Economist, London December 20, 1987.
14. Financial Times, London April 7, 1988.
15. The Independent, London June 29, 1987.
16. The Times, London June 27, 1988.

11
The Future

Many people in Pakistan and outside were pleasantly surprised when they found out after Zia's death that a constitutional procedure had been followed and the Senate Chairman, Ghulam Ishaq Khan, took over as the country's acting President. They were further relieved when the acting President announced that elections would be held on November 16, 1988, as scheduled by the late general. People also noted a glimpse of change in Government policy when Ghulam Ishaq Khan hinted at his first press conference on August 20, 1988, soon after Zia's funeral, that the elections might take place on a party basis. When reminded of Zia's statement on July 21 (1988) that the political parties would be barred from contesting national elections in November, Khan simply said: "I am not aware of any such categorical statement."

The vital question, though, was: "Why did the armed forces not take over the control of the administration in their own hands?" Not many people believed the official answer that the new army leadership (under General Aslam Baig) was genuinely interested in relinquishing power and handing it over to the civilian government. A lot has been said and written about General Aslam Baig's professionalism, and what has been described as his sincere belief that the armed forces should stay in barracks and politicians should be given charge to run the country. We do not wish to question his sincerity, but was not General Zia in 1977 described in a similar fashion? And going back a little, did the army leadership in 1971 not give the deliberate impression that the military's political role in Pakistan was over, and that they had genuinely accepted that the politicians should henceforth run the country?

Of course the circumstances were different at that time. Pakistan as a whole and the army in particular is not as demoralized now as it was after the 1971 defeat, despite the fact that with General Zia five other generals and many other senior army officers also lost their lives. But we do see at least some similarities. Most of the people in Pakistan are tired of eleven years of the Zia dictatorship. Many economic, political and social problems they see today in Pakistan, are blamed on Zia's policies. Even before Zia's death there were signs that people were losing patience with his policies, apparently designed to continue his own grip on power. In 1971 the army handed over power to a political leadership also because it feared a mass rebellion by the Pakistani people against the military, as seen two years earlier against General Ayub. At that time Zulfikar Ali Bhutto was very much alive to lead once again that rebellion. Furthermore, the military leadership was deeply divided over the causes of the Pakistani debacle in the 1971 war.

In 1988, any attempt by the army leadership to directly control the administration of the country and reimpose martial law after Zia's death could have been counter-productive. During the last few years the political leaders, particularly Benazir Bhutto, were showing signs of being able to exploit popular frustration against the military regime — thanks to General Zia himself.

Recent examples in other Asian countries, namely the Philippines, South Korea and Burma, also acted to suggest the dangers of a continuing dictatorship when people were eagerly expecting democratic rule after dictatorship. Also, there were signs of dissent in Pakistan's armed forces after Zia's death. Any action taken hurriedly could have been too costly for the army leadership. Under the circumstances, General Baig's decision appeared to be the only sensible option available to him at that time.

This does not, however, give solid grounds for optimism in the future. The political future of Pakistan depends on the combined behaviour of the military and the political leadership of the country. There is no doubt whatsoever that the military will continue to have the upper hand in the politics of Pakistan for many years to come. The military has been in power for such a long time in the country that it will be very long before a truly independent and democratic government takes office in Islamabad. The taste of power, and the privileges attached to it, would make military officers very reluctant to accept a system under which they would have to take orders from the political leadership. One has to realise that power and privileges of the military grew tremendously under Zia.

There is no doubt that much will also depend on the attitude and behaviour of the politicians. In the past the army leaders were helped by the disunity within the political opposition, and they successfully exploited their differences. Reactions of various political leaders after Zia's death have given the impression that they realize this fact. However, Zia's death has bewildered the political leaders. During his life time it was easy for them to unite against him as their single common enemy. Now they cannot help fighting each other. And the more they fight, the greater the dangers of the rapid erosion of their credibility with the people. This will simply help and encourage the military to step in.

BENAZIR FACTOR

There is only one leader in Pakistan today who has popular support at the national level, the leader of the Pakistan Peoples Party (PPP) Benazir Bhutto. There are signs that if free and fair elections take place, she would win a comfortable majority. But this very fact makes Benazir anathema to most of the establishment. Powerful military officers as well as most of those with influence in the business sector are known to detest her. Another important factor in Pakistan's future, the United States, would not be greatly happy with her victory, despite the fact that Benazir has successfully improved her relations with the U.S. in the last few years, and made carefully chosen public statements about the special relationship of Pakistan and the United States.

Indeed, some sections of Western opinion have frankly expressed their opinion in this matter. According to "The Daily Telegraph": "It is to be hoped that Pakistan's new economic well-being will rally support behind conservatives like Mr. Junejo. There is, however, a risk that General Zia's political excesses will deliver victory to Miss Benazir Bhutto . . ."[1] Yet the fact is that even a weak and humble politician like Junejo was not tolerated by the military when he started exercising a small degree of extra powers as a political leader, indicating his intention to probe matters affecting some military officers. Realizing this, another western commentator, undoubtedly representing a strand of opinion in Washington, the former National Security Adviser to President Carter, Zbigniew Brzenzinski has openly said:

"The Pakistanis should not be pressured by outsiders to move precipitously towards 'democracy', for that could actually intensify domestic tensions given the ethnic and political hatreds inherent in Pakistan . . . if the younger surviving senior officers should move to create a transitional regime, Pakistan deserves the West's sympathetic encouragement, not strident lectures."[2]

Many Pakistanis might take Brzenzinski's comments as an insult, since they seem to suggest Pakistan is not yet ready for democracy. They could argue: which country in the world is without ethnic and political tensions? And if neighbouring India can live continuously as a democracy with similar ethnic and political problems, why can't Pakistan? Brzezinski's comments sound like the similar rhetoric used by leaders of the 'free' world to justify the military

President Zia-ul-Haq's main political adversary and critic Miss Benazir Bhutto who's father, the late Prime Minister of Pakistan Zulfiqar Ali Bhutto was hanged after a prolonged and humiliating show-trial.

Photo: Courtesy of JANG, London

dictatorships of their Third World allies. Such comments are certainly not going to help improve the image of the United States and the West in Pakistan. However, there are other factors which might go against Benazir Bhutto in Pakistan. Her speeches, slogans and rhetoric are reminiscent of her father, Zulfikar Ali Bhutto, and raise similar hopes and aspirations of the people. If she comes to power, expectations will be very high and it would be really very difficult, if not impossible, for her to fulfill those expectations. The vested interests in her own party and the country at large could prove to be a major constraint. Then many observers have complained of her autocratic style and an apparent contempt for more senior and experienced leaders in the party. Moreover, her style of leadership is a very personal one, and she likes the party to follow her. Despite the PPP's mass support, the organisation is as poor as other political parties in Pakistan. This factor would make her dependent on the big landlords and people to whom her supporters at grassroot level are wary of. This dependency would make her job of fulfilling the election promises even more difficult.

However, the very idea that Benazir Bhutto might win a majority on her own is feared by most senior military officers and, thus, could become a decisive factor for the holding of the elections on time. This is precisely the reason why General Zia had been trying to avoid party-based elections. His fears, though, were personal too, as he could have been tried by a Bhutto government under the 1973 constitution for staging a coup against an elected government and even given the death sentence. Benazir has tried to be very accommodating with the military leaders since Zia's death, indicating that she had no grievances against them. However, the military is well aware that Benazir could be the most difficult of the likely elected leaders for the Generals to handle.

Ideally the military establishment would like to have either a very weak politician to be given power, who dare not question the judgments and decisions of the military officers, or an old ally whose personal interests coincide with those of the military establishment. There is no dearth of such 'leaders' in the country as many such allies of the military and business beneficiaries from the Zia regime comfortably groups themselves under the umbrella of the revived Muslim League. Such leaders, though, would hardly have any credibility with the people. Many people in Pakistan believe that the military establishment's best bet could still be the former prime minister Junejo who did achieve some popular support during his tenure. But the vested interests in the Muslim League and the military have already denied him the leadership of the party following Zia's death.

During the next few months the divisions and differences between the parties would become clearer, as well as their attitudes. In the meantime the military leadership might also sort out their differences on personal and policy issues. One thing, however, is certain. The legacy of General Zia has ensured that no civilian government can take on the military establishment. The realization of this fact could establish an alliance between a political party and the military leadership. However, there is doubt about how long such an alliance could exist, given the contradiction in the interests of the two groups and it is difficult to see such a political party also becoming popular with the masses. But since it is inconceivable to see a future political map of Pakistan without a dominant role to the military, the only option available to politicians there appears to be a broad understanding. It will not restore full democracy in the country. But it could be a beginning. There are signs that such understanding is emerging.

FOREIGN POLICY

Never before in Pakistan's history did the country's foreign policy acquire such an importance as in the Zia years. Since much of this policy revolved around the Afghan factor and General Zia himself, many observers are expecting important changes now that Zia has gone and the Afghan problem seems nearly resolved. We, however, do not anticipate any drastic changes. There is no doubt that Pakistan's geopolitical importance was beginning to recede as a result of the Geneva accord on Afghanistan and a general improvement in East-West relations. But Pakistan continues to remain important in the eyes of the United States for its key role in safeguarding western interests in the Gulf region. Precisely for this reason, Pakistan's military establishment will continue to get American support.

We also think that despite the Geneva accord, Afghanistan is likely to remain an important issue for any future government in Pakistan. This issue may not be popular with the Pakistani masses, but it would continue to be very popular with the Pakistani establishment. Despite the fact that article 5 of the Geneva accord, signed by both the Governments in Kabul and Islamabad, clearly says that Pakistan and Afghanistan shall not interfere in each other's affairs and shall not support subversion, support to Afghan Mujahideen by the Pakistan government is likely to continue. At the same time the activities of the Afghan secret service 'Khad' inside Peshawar and other parts of Pakistan could continue. However, the influence of more fundamentalist Afghan guerrilla groups is almost certainly going to decline as they can no longer expect a lion's share of all the aid distributed to Afghan Mujahideen by the Pakistani Government.

There are also external factors to influence Pakistani policy on the Afghan issue. The United States is likely to press Pakistan to continue support to the Mujahideen until at least all the Soviet forces are returned home. The absence of Zia might encourage the Soviets to harden their attitude about the future leadership of Kabul. This could prolong the Afghan war. The historic rivalry with Afghanistan and India is also likely to encourage any Pakistani leadership in continuing its active support to the Mujahideen. We also do not foresee any major improvement in Pakistan's ties with India until India's Punjab problem is controlled, and an elected regime comes to power in Islamabad. Similarly, any new Pakistani Government is likely to maintain close relations with the Islamic world and China.

The successors of Zia, though, are not likely to have as smooth time with the West as before. The absence of Zia's strong personality, together with the reduced importance of the Afghan issue, will effectively curtail the bargaining position of the new government. Pakistan's nuclear programme and the extent of drug trafficking are likely to provoke renewed tensions in relations. These combined issues could soon make Western aid to Pakistan really conditional, particularly if a Democratic administration comes to power in the forthcoming American elections.

Pakistan's economic prospects are also looking far from bright. The most important source of foreign exchange during the Zia years – remittances from Pakistanis working in the Gulf – has already lost importance. The glut in the oil market in the recent past has produced constraints on the Gulf economies, and many expatriate workers have already returned home. This factor has not only affected the Pakistani revenues, but also increases dangers of unemployment. Lack of investment during the Zia regime is also going to multiply the economic problems.

Apart from some major disturbances in Sind (in 1983) and recent ethnic clashes in Karachi, the provinces remained unusually calm under Zia. The underlying frustrations in these provinces could create serious problems for the government. As discussed in the previous chapter, the Afghan problem overshadowed the existing political and economic issues under Zia in the Frontier province. The new government will have to face these problems now that the Afghan issue is receding. There are also likely to be more tensions between the refugees and the host population over demands for refugees' return to Afghanistan. Baluchistan is already sitting on a volcano. The continued domination of Baluchis by Punjabis and the heavy presence of the armed forces in the province give signs of the seriousness of the problem. The frustration of the Baluchi people also lies in the fact that most of their political leadership is either living in exile, or bitterly divided over the strategy to fight with the establishment in Islamabad and the extent of autonomy for their province.

The situation in Sind, particularly in the capital city of Karachi also gives cause for serious concern. The main problem in the province itself is similar to Baluchistan, that is, unsatisfied demands for more autonomy. This is also a province in which agitations have been blamed on Indian interference by the Pakistani government. The real problem, however has arisen from the feeling of discrimination within the Sindhi population against Punjabi and alien domination. This problem is likely to continue until there is a fundamental rethinking on the part of the military establishment, and a consensus that the future of Pakistan cannot be secured until people in the various provinces are given wider autonomy.

Karachi, of course, is a different problem. This city, which is also Pakistan's biggest, is dominated by people from all the various ethnic communities. In fact, Sindhis here are now in a minority. This is said to be enough ground for the Sindhis to feel resentment against whom they consider as outsiders. Recently there has been a continuous tension between two sizable ethnic groups in the city – the Pushtuns (Pathans) and the Mohajirs. During the last few years of Zia regime, this city had seen some of the most violent clashes between these two groups. The easy availability of guns, thanks to Afghan factor, has played an important part in these clashes. Zia regime failed to solve this problem and as result the tension had grown considerably. Some Pakistanis fear that the situation in Karachi, if not controlled, could easily develop itself like that in Beirut, in view of the passions raised, and the continued efforts by the rival communities to arm themselves to prepare themselves for full-scale armed conflict. This problem could also become a major headache for any future government in Pakistan.

Thus, the immediate future of Pakistan, unfortunately, does not look very optimistic. There appears to be an earnest desire amongst people for a democratic set-up in the country. But they cannot be sure about the real intentions of their military rulers. These never handed over power willingly to elected politicians except in 1971. Will they make another exception, or hold on? There may well be senior officers in the army with genuine intentions to let politicians run their country. But will they be able to restrain some of the more ambitious officers in their ranks holding very different ideas? And, will politicians like Benazir Bhutto really succeed in removing the apprehensions of the military and its obstinate foreign supporters (such as Brzenzinski), and, not least, their political foes in Baluchistan and Frontier, that once in power they would not forget these minority interests. Only time can give the correct answers to these vital questions.

THE FUTURE

We do, however, think that only a clear understanding between the military and politicians, and their responsible behaviour towards the people of Pakistan, can pave the way towards a democratic future of the country.

1. Leader in "The Daily Telegraph", London, 19.8.88.
2. In an article to "The Times", London, 26.8.88.

Appendix A

General Mohammad Zia-ul-Haq's First Address to the Nation: 5th July 1977

I deem it a singular honour to address the great nation of this great country. I am grateful to God Almightly for this. You must have learnt by now that the Government of Mr Zulfikar Ali Bhutto has ceased to exist and an interim Government has been established in its place. This change-over which began at about midnight last night, was completed by this morning. I am grateful to God Almighty that the process of change-over has been accomplished smoothly and peacefully. This action was carried out on my orders. During this period the former Prime Minister Zulfikar Ali Bhutto and some of his colleagues have been taken into protective custody. Likewise, all the prominent leaders of the Pakistan National Alliance except Begum Nasim Wali Khan have also been taken in to custody.

The reactions to this takeover have so far been very encouraging. A stream of congratulatory messages has been pouring in from different quarters. I am grateful for this to my nation as well as to the buoyant and "Momin" Armed Forces of Pakistan.

It is necessary to add here that some people have expressed misgiving that the Army takeover may have been at the behest of someone. Could it be that General Zia had secretly concerted with the former Prime Minister? On this, I can only say that truth can never remain unexposed. In fact, such an air of distrust has been created during the past few months that even well-meaning people also get bogged down in doubts and apprehensions.

You must have heard from the morning news bulletin that the Armed Forces of Pakistan have taken over the administration of the country. The Army takeover is never a pleasant act, because the Armed Forces of Pakistan genuinely want that the administration of the country should remain in the hands of the representatives of the people who are its real masters. The people exercise this right through their elected representatives, who are chosen in every democratic country through periodic elections.

The elections were held in our beloved homeland on March 7 last. The election results, however, were rejected by one of the contending parties (the Pakistan National Alliance). They alleged that the elections had been rigged on a large scale and demanded fresh elections. To press their demand for re-elections, they launched a movement which assumed such dimensions that people even started saying that democracy was not workable in Pakistan. But I genuinely feel that the survival of this country lies in democracy and democracy alone.

It is mainly due to this belief that the Armed Forces resisted the temptation to take over during the recent provocative circumstances in spite of diverse massive political pressures. The Armed Forces have always desired and tried for the political solution to political problems. That is why the Armed Forces stressed on the then Government that they should reach a compromise with their political rivals without any loss of time. The Government needed time to hold these talks. The Armed forces bought them this valuable period of time by maintaining law and order in the country. The Armed Forces were subjected to criticism from certain quarters for their role in aid of the civil administration, but we tolerated this criticism in the hope that it was a passing phase. We hoped that when this climate of agitational frenzy came to an end, the nation would be able to appreciate the correct and constitutional role of the Armed Forces and all fears would be allayed.

I have just given you a very broad outline picture of the situation obtaining in the country. It must be quite clear to you now that when the political leaders failed to steer the country out of a crisis, it is an inexcusable sin for the Armed Forces to sit as silent spectators. It is primarily, for this reason, that the Army perforce, had to intervene, to save the country.

I would like to point out here that I saw no prospects of a compromise between the People's Party and the PNA, because of their mutual distrust and lack of faith. It was feared that the failure of the PNA and PPP to reach a compromise would throw the country into chaos and the country would thus be plunged into a more serious crisis. This risk could not be taken in view of the larger interest of the country. The Army had, therefore, to act as a result of which the Government of Mr Bhutto has ceased to exist: Martial Law has been imposed throughout the country; the National and Provincial Assemblies have been dissolved and the provincial Governors and Ministers have been removed.

But the Constitution has not been abrogated. Only the operation of certain parts of the Constitution has been held in abeyance. Mr Fazal Elahi Chaudhry has very kindly consented to continue to discharge his duties as President of Pakistan as heretofore under the same Constitution. I am grateful to him for this. To assist him in the discharge of his national duties, a four-member Military Council has been formed. The Council consists of the Chairman, Joint Chiefs of Staff, and Chiefs of Staff of the Army, Navy and Air Force.

I will discharge the duties of the Chief Martial Law Administrator. Martial Law orders and instructions, as and when required, will be issued under my orders.

I met Mr Justice Yaqub Ali, Chief Justice of Pakistan, this morning. I am grateful to him for the advice and guidance on legal matters. I want to make it absolutely clear that neither I have any political ambitions nor does the Army want to be detracted from its profession of soldiering. I was obliged to step in to fill in the vacuum created by the political leaders. I have accepted this challenge as a true soldier of Islam. My sole aim is to organise free and fair elections which would be held in October this year.

Soon after the polls, power will be transferred to the elected representatives of the people. I give a solemn assurance that I will not deviate from this schedule. During the next three months, my total attention will be concentrated on the holding of elections and I would not like to dissipate my powers and energies as Chief Martial Law Administrator on anything else.

It will not be out of place to mention here that I hold the Judiciary of the country in high esteem. I will do my best to refrain from doing anything which is likely to restrict the power of the Judiciary. However, under unavoidable circumstances, if and when Martial Law Orders and Martial Law Regulations are issued they would not be challenged in any court of law.

I will soon announce the modalities and detailed timetable for the holding of elections. I hope and expect that all political parties will co-operate with me in this behalf. A good measure of tension had been created in the country during the recent political confrontation. It had, therefore, become imperative to allow time to cool off human emotions. I have, therefore, banned all political activities from today till further orders. Political activities, however, will be allowed before the polls.

My dear countrymen, I have expressed my real feelings and intentions, without the slightest ambiguity. I have also taken you into confidence about my future plans. I seek guidance from God Almighty and help and co-operation from my countrymen to achieve this noble mission. I also hope that the Judiciary, the administration and the common man will extend wholehearted co-operation to me.

It would be my utmost endeavour to ensure that the Martial Law Administration not only treats the people in a spirit of justice and equality but also make them feel so. The civil administration, too, had to play an important role in this behalf. I am, therefore, pleased to announce that the Chief Justices of the Provincial High Courts have, on my request, consented to become the Acting Governors of their respective provinces. The officers in the civil administration, who have any apprehensions about their future, are hereby assured that no victimisation will take place.

However, if any public servant fails in the discharge of his duties, shows partial role or betrays the confidence of the nation, he will be given exemplary punishment. Similarly, if any citizen disturbs law and order in the country he will also be severely dealt with.

So far as foreign relations are concerned, I want to make it absolutely clear that I will honour all the agreements, commitments and contracts signed by the outgoing Government.

In the end, I would appeal to all the officers and men of the Armed Forces to discharge their duties justly and impartially. I hope they will deal with every situation without showing any undue lenience. I will also expect them to forgive those who have ridiculed or harassed them. This will be in the true Islamic tradition. I call upon them to preserve their own honour and that of their profession in the discharge of their duties. I am sure they will acquit themselves of their new responsibility honourably. This will certainly enhance their prestige and position in the society.

I will now like to enumerate the following few points:-

1. The civil courts will continue to discharge their duties as before.
2. The Federal Security Force will soon be reorganised.
3. Large-scale transfers of civil servants, which have been ordered recently, will be reviewed.
4. The organisation of the Interim Government is as follows:
   (a) President Fazal Elahi Chaudhry will be the Head of the State.
   (b) The important administrative matters will be dealt with by the Military Council mentioned earlier.
   (c) The Chief Martial Law Administrator will be the Chief Executive.
   (d) Secretary-General Defence, Mr Ghulam Ishaq Khan, will co-ordinate the functioning of all Federal Ministries and Departments.
   (e) The Federal Secretaries will continue to head their respective departments.
   (f) The Chief Justices of the provincial High Courts will be the Acting Governors of their respective provinces.
   (g) The Provincial Administration will be headed by the Provincial Martial

Law Administrators, and the Provincial Secretaries will continue to hold charge of their respective departments.

5. I sincerely desire:-
   (a) The Civil administration to discharge its duties without any fear or apprehension.
   (c) The Press to live up to its claims as the advocate of "freedom of the Press" without violating the "code of conduct".
   (d) The nation to develop a sense of sanity and reasonableness.
   (e) The life, honour and property of every citizen to be safe.
   (f) Peace and tranquillity to prevail and 'Goondaism' to come to an end, and,
   (g) Educational institutions not be become political arenas.
6. I want to assure you that the frontiers of Pakistan are fully guarded and the Armed Forces are there to discharge their duties. Authorised traffic across the borders is continuing.
7. To conclude, I must say that the spirit of Islam, demonstrated during the recent movement, was commendable. It proves that Pakistan, which was created in the name of Islam will continue to survive only if it sticks to Islam. That is why, I consider the introduction of Islamic system as an essential pre-requisite for the country.

Pakistan Paindabad.

Appendix B

KEY ECONOMIC A SOCIAL INDICATORS OF SAARC (1985)

	Bangla-Desh	Bhutan	Nepal	India	Pakistan	Sri Lanka	Low Income Economies
Area (000 Sq Km)	144	47	141	3288	804	66	32547
Population (mln.) in mid-1985	100.6	1.2	16.5	765.1	96.2	15.8	2439.4
Crude Birth Rate (per thousand)	40	43	43	33	44	25	29
Crude Death Rate (per thousand)	15	21	18	12	15	6	10
Life expectancy at birth (years)	51	44	47	56	51	70	60
Per Capita:							
i) GNP ($)	150	160	160	270	380	380	270
ii) Energy Consumption (KOE)	41	..	49	30	52	33	32
iii) Daily Calorie Supply	1899	2571	2034	2189	2159	2385	2339
Terms of Trade (1980=100)	113	..	94	115	95	97	94
Gross International Reserves (in months of import Coverage)	1.4	..	2.2	5.4	2.2	2.2	4.1
Average Annual rate of inflation (%)	11.5	..	8.4	7.8	8.1	14.7	7.5
Average Annual Growth Rate (%) (1980-85):							
i) GDP	3.6	..	3.4	5.2	6.0	5.1	7.3
ii) Agriculture	2.8	..	..	2.7	2.1	4.0	6.0
iii) Manufacturing	2.0	..	..	5.6	10.1	5.5	10.8
iv) Merchandise Exports (FOB)	7.1	..	8.4	4.6	2.4	7.3	5.0
v) Merchandise Imports (CIF)	3.1	..	7.8	2.2	3.9	1.5	7.3
vi) GNP Per Capita (65-85)	0.4	..	0.1	1.7	2.6	2.9	2.9

.. Not Available   Source: World Development Report, 1987.

Appendix C

PUBLIC SECTOR EXPENDITURE

(Rs. million)

Sector	First Plan (1955-60)	Second Plan (1960-65)	Third Plan (1965-70)	Non-Plan Period (1970-78)	Fifth Plan (1978-83)	Sixth Plan Allocations (1983-88)	Sixth Plan (1983-88) (R.E.)
Agriculture	461	902	1,377	4,692	14,860	15,350	18,018
(a) Agriculture	461	695	822	4,141	6,060	12,350	7,876
(b) Fertilizer Subsidy	–	207	555	2,351	8,800	3,000	10,142
Water	969	4,597	4,513	12,810	15,770	32,100	23,641
Energy	607	1,293	1,760	13,841	38,830	116,500	58,968
(a) Power	757	1,165	1,571	10,880	28,119	87,400	46,712
(b) Fuels	32	128	189	2,961	11,711	29,100	12,256
Industry	742	478	786	11,294	25,400	20,500	5,340
Minerals	124	94	271	492	400	5,750	1,098
Transport and Communications	1,080	1,595	2,521	15,653	35,210	57,520	27,099
Physical Planning and Housing	505	957	698	5,687	9,000	15,500	17,581
Education and Manpower	232	463	563	3,442	5,640	19,850	14,519
Health	76	174	281	2,381	4,580	13,000	10,771
Population Welfare Programme	–	9	145	820	600	2,300	2,000
Other/Miscellaneous Programmes	67	44	289	2,632	2,320	6,630	14,147
Sub-Total:	4,863	10,606	13,204	75,544	152,610	305,000	193,122
Plus: Special Development Programme	–	–	–	–	150	15,000	3,571
Less: Operational Shorfall	–	–	–	–	–	30,000	–
Total (Net):	4,863	10,606	13,204	75,544	152,760	290,000	196,693

– nil.
R.E. Revised estimates.

Source: Planning and Development Division.
Govt. of Pakistan.

137